Praise from Six Continents
WE the Change

"Brilliant! Genius! Necessary! Shannon has the uncanny ability to take an amorphous subject like Change Management and give it form and structure. I could have really used Shannon's guidance when, in my thirties, a divorce necessitated that I get off my butt, visualize the life I wanted, and create that life. This is a must-read for anyone feeling stuck and not knowing what the first step in changing their situation should be. Kudos to Shannon for creating a playbook for pilgrims walking their own Camino de Santiago."

— *Connie Pate, EdD, retired partner,*
Strawn Arnold & Associates, North America

"*WE the Change* is an invitation to all of us women who hesitate about our own ability and potential. The book gently nudges us to step out of our comfort zone and take the plunge. This book is a gift for all women who are exploring their own leadership and want to express it in their own authentic way. It is one of those rare books that I would keep on my bedside and open on a difficult day, knowing that it will provide me the guidance I need at that moment."

— *Eeran Chawla, Google, OD practitioner,*
APAC, India, Asia

"In *WE the Change*, Shannon Wallis packs a lifetime of experience coaching business leaders around the world, into an inspiring, authentic, and practical approach anyone can apply to their lives and careers. If you are not sure how to create what you want . . . or if you are not sure what it is you precisely want . . . this book will set you on the path and arm you with the conviction and passion to see it through."

— *Kaihan Krippendorff, founder of Outthinker and author*
of Driving Innovation from Within, North America

"Through her captivating book, Shannon is right by your side, connecting with your struggles as she details her grueling 500-mile Camino trek as a metaphor for change. Drawing on her deep expertise as a corporate transformation coach, she offers the tools you need to get unstuck and succeed."

— *Sanyin Siang, Thinkers50 #1 leadership coach and*
author of The Launch Book, North America

"I can't help but wonder how much braver I would have been in life if I had read Shannon's book as a young woman in my twenties. Her personal story is captivating and compelling. I was SO inspired by her courage— all the practical tips were an added bonus! *WE the Change* is a how-to manual for living your best life!"
— *Kimberly Faith, award-winning author of Your Lion Inside, systems thinking expert, and futurist, North America*

"Shannon shares deeply personal and challenging times of her life where she overcame adversity and she gives her readers highly practical and relevant advice along with exercises to help find their calling in life. I could not put Shannon's captivating book down and highly recommend it for anyone that wants to be inspired, learn and become their best selves. *WE the Change* is an inspiring and powerful must-read."
— *Sabina Nawaz, Global CEO coach, writer for Harvard Business Review and Forbes, and ex-Microsoft executive, Canada, North America*

"Shannon convinces us 'I can, you can, together we can.' This is a book for me, my daughter, my clients, and all the Chinese females who are on the Camino to discover and realize their full potential. Our challenges and obstacles are as real as the scorching sun, the rainy days, and the hard road. We share the same fatigue, anxiety, and fear. *WE the Change* provides a clear and inspiring vision of what we truly want for our lives and helps us to take the first step with faith. Trust me, reading this book will guide you there."
— *Karen Zong, managing director at Integrated Development Group, Hong Kong, SAR China, Asia*

"I was immediately connected to Shannon's story after reading the first pages of *WE the Change*. Her book is an invitation for self-discovery and growing consciousness. Shannon's heartfelt narrative is an act of courage and compassion. It helps unfold our inner capabilities to drive deep change."
— *Izabel Cortez, Human Resources, GE Renewable Energy, Brazil, South America*

"Shannon Wallis' years of experience as an organizational change consultant, leadership coach, and spiritual guide have coalesced in *WE the Change* to create a model for personal and professional transformation. Her authenticity, vulnerability, and humility deliver a message of hope while her simple framework makes big change believable and doable. I will be recommending this book to all women and men I coach seeking to be and WE their full potential."
— *Sarita Soldz, executive coach, Career Services, University of Virginia Darden School of Business, North America*

"Timeless, profound, personal, and moving. A superb weave of trials and tribulations, philosophy and practice. WE the Change propels us into our greatness, revealing the essential steps to make our change, impactful, enduring, and epic."
— **Ben Faranda, leadership coach and consultant, Queensland, Australia**

"Shannon Wallis has provided an important guide for those of us who want to make the world a better place. Starting with her belief in the power of women to make change, and sharing the wisdom of her personal journey, she places a roadmap in our hands. This is a must-read for those who believe in the power of one person to change the world."
— **Constance F. Kane, PhD, executive director, Empowered to Educate, North America**

"WE the Change is a wonderful offering of practical steps to take toward vision and change, with an understanding that God is always with us to be our guide. It is a message of hope, healing, and inspiration for us all."
— **Karen Johnson, senior associate at Centered.org and founder of the Take Root podcast, North America**

"WE the Change is truly an inspirational book. This is a great read."
— **Stephen E. Sass, partner, engagement manager, founder, CoachSource, LLC, North America**

"WE the Change encouraged me to look for ways to change my life for the better. I felt hopeful and empowered after reading it. The strategies Shannon offers can help us all become our best selves."
— **Dr. Beth Cabrera, author of Beyond Happy: Women, Work, and Well-Being, North America**

"I could not put Shannon's captivating book down and highly recommend it for anyone that wants to be inspired, learn, and become their best selves. WE the Change is an inspiring and powerful must-read."
— **Ana White, EVP and chief people officer at F5 Networks, North America**

"WE the Change combines the simple steps of creating vision with the challenges of daily living that keep many of us from moving our dreams forward. After more than thirty years in leadership, I find WE the Change a refreshing reminder to never give up on a vision and assess and embrace dissatisfaction to keep us moving forward."
— **Jenny Lockwald-Stewart, executive director, Trinity Education Foundation, North America**

"*WE the Change* is part memoir, part call to action. An inspiring book filled with insights and actions to accomplish transformative change in our lives."
— *Karen Wilson, partner, Guidehouse, North America*

"Shannon Wallis' recipe for transformational change works! I was fortunate enough to have her as a coach. With openness and humility, she grounds each chapter of *WE the Change* by weaving the powerful story of her pilgrimage to El Camino de Santiago with real-life lessons for creating your own successful hero's journey. I highly recommend this book for helping you break through and create your personal future."
— *Kathryn McKinley, principal research scientist, Google, North America*

"*WE the Change* is a heartwarming and inspirational story of a remarkable woman's journey through life and along the Camino. Shannon's exceptional coaching SKILLS and instincts emerge throughout the book, offering POWERFUL tools and STRATEGIES that will resonate with WOMEN of all ages."
— *Lindsey Keiter Mangone, VIP and VOC Product for Mobile Games, Amazon, North America*

"Shannon Wallis' book is jammed with inspiration and packed with creative ideas. As the founder of a non-profit organization which serves the special needs population, my mind was opened by Shannon's work to new and exciting solutions. I truly wish I had had it as a resource during my twenty-three years serving in the US Navy. I will be counting on and referring to this gift for years to come."
— *Mary Borojevich, founder, SNAP (Special Needs Advocacy Partners), North America*

"Shannon Wallis takes us through a marvelous journey of self-reflection and provides a practical guide for those of us who have passion for leadership."
— *Gianna Soto, senior manager, EEWOC, Amazon Web Services, North America*

the Change

LAUNCHING BIG IDEAS AND
CREATING NEW REALITIES

SHANNON WALLIS

IGNITE
PRESS
Fresno, CA

Published in the United States by
Ignite Press
5070 N 6th St. #189
Fresno, CA 93710
www.IgnitePress.us

ISBN: 978-1-953655-45-5 (Amazon Print)

ISBN: 978-1-953655-46-2 (IngramSpark) PAPERBACK

ISBN: 978-1-953655-47-9 (IngramSpark) HARDCOVER

ISBN: 978-1-953655-48-6 (E-book)

For bulk purchase and for booking, contact:
Shannon Wallis

Shannon@CascadeLeadership.Solutions, https://wethechange.solutions

Because of the dynamic nature of the Internet, web addresses or links contained in this book may have been changed since publication and may no longer be valid. The content of this book and all expressed opinions are those of the author and do not reflect the publisher or the publishing team.

The author is solely responsible for all content included herein.

The characters and all stories in this book are real. The names of the individuals have been used with their permission or changed to protect their privacy.

Library of Congress Control Number: 2021900004

Cover design by Umair Tariq
Edited by Emma Hatcher
Interior design by Michelle White
"Camino de Santiago" map courtesy of iStockPhoto
"Productive Dialogue" image adapted with permission from
"Difficult Conversations" by Erik Mazziotta

Other Books **Shannon Wallis** has Contributed to

Advancing Human Resource Project Management by Richard J. Klimoski, Beverly A. Dugan, Carla Messikomer, and François Chiocchio

Experience-Driven Leader Development: Models, Tools, Best Practices, and Advice for On-the-Job Development by Cynthia D. McCauley, D. Scott DeRue, Paul R. Yost, and Sylvester Taylor

Coaching for Leadership: Writings on Leadership from the World's Greatest Coaches, Third Edition by Marshall Goldsmith, Laurence S. Lyons, and Sarah McArthur

Best Practices in Talent Management: How the World's Leading Organizations Manage, Develop, and Retain Top Talent by Marshall Goldsmith and Louis Carter

Blueprint for Success: Proven Strategies for Success & Survival by Frank A. Prince, Stephen Covey, and Ken Blanchard

For my Lovelies, Savannah Joy and Fiona Shirí,
and
Patricia Ann Gray, the original Lovely.

ACKNOWLEDGMENTS

A tribe of supporters has contributed their spirit and energy to making *WE the Change* a reality. First and foremost, my family. When I ventured into writing a book, evenings, weekends, and even vacations were affected. My husband, Joe, exemplifies one of the central messages of *WE the Change*. Generosity of spirit supports and connects people, enabling new realities to be born. I have learned through his mastery and am grateful to be his partner in enabling people to realize their full professional potential. Savannah and Fiona, you are the inspiration for this book. Your compassion, creativity, and collaboration exemplify the change I wish to see in the world. Thank you, Joe, Savannah, and Fiona for understanding how important the book is to me and providing the space and continuity to complete it. In addition, I thank my parents, Patricia, Michael, and Maryellen. While our family life wasn't always a walk in the park, it formed me and I wouldn't change it. My compassion and resilience comes from you. I am profoundly grateful to witness the transformation each of you have achieved in your own lives. As an adult, I have a greater appreciation for the personal "Caminos" each of you has experienced.

A small yet powerful team helped to move this book to completion. I wouldn't have a book without Marcia Zina Mager, my writing coach. A coach's coach, she was a confidante, supporter, and occasional therapist as she helped me to let go of the voices in my head in order to put my ideas on paper. I am deeply grateful for Marcia's generosity, persistence, spirit, and great sense of humor throughout the experience of writing my book. Cindy Healy championed my

Camino story from the first time she heard it, engaging me to speak at multiple Microsoft events and DigiGirlz, as well as joining me for my second Camino. She continually encouraged me to tell my story and volunteered her team for a two-day workshop to support my first approach to writing the book. Jordan Hoglund, my intern, read the entire draft and tested every exercise. She pointed out what inspired and moved her and the places that required more work in order to be truly useful. Sean Maher arrived in the final hour and provided valuable contributions that a poet would recognize. Each person has made a lasting and unique contribution to *WE the Change*.

The pilgrims who accompanied me on the Camino deserve their own mention. Unbeknownst to each, they joined me for periods of time as I remembered and wrote about my experience. I'd hear their words of reflection and encouragement and transfer them to the page. I am grateful for your wisdom: from Camino One—Susan Severn and Lori Key; from Camino Two—Erin Aitken, Michele "Miki" Bell, Sheri O'Neill, and Susie Buysse.

Preparation for this book started many years before I finally wrote it. Specific moments of insight generated in the presence of the following supporters have made their way into *WE the Change*. Thank you to Amanda Ridder, Asli Aker, Carmen White, Carol Rice, Debbie Ridder, Doug Wallace, EMM, Encarnacion Wallis, Erik Mazziotta, Holly Sider Smith, Jacob Maher, Julie Maloney, Justin Maher, Kaihan Krippendorff, Kimberly Faith, Kristina Maher, LeAnne Gallagher, Lisa Finn, Louie Spivak, Maria Russell, Mark Smith, Paul O'Beirne, Virginia "Prinny" Anderson, Sabina Nawaz, Sarita Soldz, Shannon Banks, Sherry Bisaillon, Suzanne White, Tara Cherechinsky, Tony Crabbe, and Ursula Carrion. In addition, thank you to the team at Ignite Press. Everett O'Keefe, Malia Sexton, Emma Hatcher, and Chris Simmons, your expertise during the publishing period calmed my nerves. Thank you for being a part of the journey and for the opportunity to learn from you.

TABLE OF CONTENTS

INTRODUCTION

In 2002, I embarked on a life-changing journey. I walked El Camino de Santiago, a 500-mile medieval footpath and pilgrimage route crossing northern Spain which has beckoned thousands of pilgrims annually for over a thousand years. In the years since I walked the Camino, it has become increasingly apparent to me that my life is about being of service: I consider myself to be a messenger of hope, agent of transformation, guardian of the innocent, mother to the Lovelies, and guide for *WE the Change*. Each one of these roles holds special meaning which I reveal in the conclusion. My personal narrative of change and overcoming adversity, along with my professional experience of guiding change within organizations like Coca-Cola and Microsoft, causes people to seek me out for my perspective and advice. I find that result both humbling and filled with responsibility. I could have written this book in myriad ways in the past eighteen years since the Camino, but not just any way would have worked. If you're willing to listen, I want the message to be of value, to uplift you, and to contribute to your ability to reach your full potential.

Today, my vision is to help eradicate poverty in some small way, shape, or form and to help others to find their voice. The book targets young women because they have not always had the same guidance or opportunities as our young men. In addition, if we look around our global community, we observe that children living in poverty are disproportionately in single family homes headed by women, many of whom have ideas that, if put into action, could transform their families' lives as well as their own.

One of the women with ideas is my mother. When I was eleven years old, my parents divorced. My father's day-to-day absence created a precarious position. My mother could only find a minimum-wage job. Her income covered the mortgage on a modest home, but very little else. We received government assistance for heat, food, and healthcare. As a middle-school girl, the change devastated me, but I carried hope. My mother was an amazing artist who specialized in drawing children and characters. She routinely made drawings for friends and created her own cards. Often, she talked about launching a line of cards, and this diamond of an idea kept hope alive in me. One day, my mother would hit it big and our problems would be over. She had beautiful plans for what we would do with the money. Beyond taking care of all of our needs, she'd create a company called God's Shop, where people just like us could shop without paying for the household items they would need. She thought beyond us. She thought big. She thought of making a difference.

Unfortunately, the line of cards and God's Shop never came to pass. Like so many women before her, my mother was riddled with fear, self-doubt, and a belief that her ideas—and she herself—just weren't good enough. She couldn't see a step-by-step way out. She didn't know how to start. She quit before beginning. It's hard to self-actualize when you are fighting for basic survival needs like food, clothing, and shelter. I went to college precisely because my mother looked at me one day and said, "Shannon, never let this happen to you. Get an education."

I believe my mother's inability to claim her rightful path and realize her full potential ends with me. I represent what she could not achieve for herself. I have achieved the professional success she hoped to, and I am realizing my full potential. But I view this shift in circumstances as tenuous. I have other family members who suffer as my mother did. What is different about me or my approach that enabled me to make my dreams come true? More importantly, I fear that, if I don't codify it, it could be lost to my own daughters. By writing it down and understanding it, I believe my Lovelies, my daughters (both literal and figurative), will have a formula to realize their potential.

This book is meant to help women who, like my mother, have the desire to launch a Big Idea or create a New Reality for themselves, their families, and others. Gandhi said, to create change, "Be the change you wish to see in the world." As I reflect on my own practice to "be the change," I realize that I do this best when I work with others. Women tend to be more adept at building community and working collectively to get things done. With a roadmap and our relationships, we are more likely to *"WE the Change"* to realize our individual and collective dreams. Together, *Women Empower the Change*; together, we are more able to launch our Big Ideas and create our New Realities. May this book act as that roadmap and guide you to achieve success.

AN INVITATION

Think of it like this: Here we are, girlfriend to girlfriend, over a coffee, tea, or a glass of wine, talking it through (oh, and let's not forget the chocolate because I like chocolate—dark chocolate). Like you, I want to create new things and/or see my ideas take hold. You tell me, "I have this idea for a new podcast. How do I start? How do I make it happen?" Or maybe you share:

"I've been asked to lead a new product launch at work. I don't know where to start and I feel like I'm in over my head! What was my boss thinking, asking me to do this?"

"Really?!" I exclaim, "Awesome, just the type of challenge I'm up for! I have an approach that requires some effort, but it works, and I'd love to guide you on your journey, if you're open to it."

I've been doing this type of work for more than twenty years from corporations like Coca-Cola and Microsoft to NGOs like United Planet and Nuestros Pequeños Hermanos. I'd launched many Big Ideas, created several New Realities, and driven multiple transformational changes before I even codified my approach; simply put, it's in my DNA. I've guided thousands of individuals and leaders across six continents, with employee sizes ranging from fifteen to more than a million, in this approach. We've worked on individual challenges, such as becoming a better manager or leader, managing time more effectively, and getting accepted to medical school, and collective challenges, such as launching a new development program, creating a non-profit, and globally scaling a business service. I know quite a bit about it.

Can I share it with you? Anything is possible if you just say yes. What do you say?

HOW THE BOOK IS ORGANIZED

The book has two parts. Part One is my Camino story. Through personal storytelling and reflection, it examines a time in my life when I had a Big Idea and how I managed to accomplish it. It includes eleven chapters, each with two sections.

The first section tells the story of my Big Idea. The second section expresses the lesson I learned, my current understanding of this lesson, and what I have learned since. Part Two is the workbook. It guides you through practical application of the lessons. It provides exercises to support *your* endeavor, your Big Idea or New Reality. It answers questions such as: How do you turn the inspiration for an idea into reality? How do you not only start but also (and more importantly) create enough momentum to complete what you started? The chapters and exercises follow the same sequence as in Part One. They provide a set of first steps that are embedded in my preferred approach to change. I don't profess that these set of exercises will address all of your questions, but I believe they will answer many.

USING THIS SELF-GUIDED COACHING PROCESS

The book is written in the spirit of my coaching practice. To use it for self-guided coaching, I recommend the following approach: Read the Camino story completely to understand the story and approach. Next, read it again, chapter by chapter. After reading each chapter, work with the exercises in the parallel chapters found in the workbook. Chapter by chapter, you will create the plan to launch your Big Idea or create your New Reality. Of course, don't feel locked into this approach. If you discover another way that suits you better, use that. Whichever you choose . . .

Let's begin.

PART ONE

WE THE CHANGE: LAUNCHING BIG IDEAS AND CREATING NEW REALITIES

ONE
THE CALL

Why would anyone, especially someone who is not an avid hiker, strap on a twenty-pound pack with just one change of clothes and two sets of underwear, walk through mountains and wheat fields in northern Spain, in pouring rain and scorching sun, through heartbreak and despair, and then search for lodging, water, and food every day for thirty days? The answer is "a vision." I had a vision—a calling—that was so compelling, I could not say no. And, it was one of the most significant learning experiences in my life, both personally and professionally, because it taught me what it really takes to achieve our dreams and to get to our destinations. It wasn't academic theory written in a book about change management. The lessons were real, personal, and profound.

After several years on the road as a bi-coastal management consultant specializing in organizational change, I burned out. I left the external consulting world and joined Coca-Cola as an internal consultant, hoping the grind would slow down. It still found me. After two years at Coke, I realized it was me, not the work, that had to change, and I applied for a leadership development program, *Leading with Spirit*, which convened four times in California over the course of one year. I have a strong spiritual foundation, and I hoped that I would learn what it would mean for me to Lead with Spirit. I was *thrilled when I was accepted to the program and grateful Coke would pay the tuition and expenses for me. During the third program retreat in June 1999, I received "the call." Walking through the woods, I suddenly stopped in front of a large evergreen. Did it "wave" to me? I blinked. I couldn't move—I was rooted to the path. Light broke through the branches and communicated with me. I didn't specifically hear it, but I suddenly knew: I would go to northern Spain to do "something" spiritual. The meaning of "something" wasn't clear—I didn't understand it. Nonetheless, I felt compelled to answer the call. After the retreat, I flew home to Atlanta, and I said to my husband of two months, "Joe, we're moving to Spain."*

I'll never forget his look of brief confusion as if he hadn't heard me correctly.

"I can't explain it, but I have to go to Spain—northern Spain—to do something spiritual. I think it will be in October."

Joe grew up in a military family, attended the US Naval Academy, and was a marine officer. At that point in time, he was a reservist enjoying his post-active duty military career at Accenture. While many of my friends would later comment that their husbands would never leave their own careers to support those of their wives, Joe didn't bat an eye. He didn't question my desire or complain about how it might affect his career; he supported me. With his okay, my journey to Santiago had begun.

LESSON ONE
Anything Is Possible If You Just Say Yes

What if I hadn't taken the call seriously? What if I had decided it was some trick of my mind, some foolishness? What if Joe hadn't been supportive? *What if . . . What if . . . What if . . . ?* For a person with an imagination, life has many *what ifs*. My mom's cards and God's Shop were *what ifs*. Without a plan to achieve them, the *what ifs* often become *only ifs*: If only I'd done _____, I wouldn't feel dissatisfied, dismay, despair, unfulfilled, or possibly find myself living in poverty. I don't have much patience for unimplemented *what ifs* or their sisters, *only ifs*. Somewhere along my life path, I made an unconscious decision; I would say *yes* to Big Ideas and figure out how to achieve them. I discovered that many things, almost anything, became possible when I did those two things.

While this wasn't the first time I had heeded a call, it may have been the first time I was conscious I had been called *and* decided to say yes. Prior to this call, I had spent many years manifesting my clients' Big Ideas, creating what I think of as New Realities, or what others might call transformational change. Often, these projects required several months, and sometimes years, to complete. The timeframe and steps to complete the project can sound daunting to a beginner, but it can be simplified to three phases:

1. Define what you want.
2. Understand where you are starting and what might be getting in the way.
3. Take steps to close the gap between the first two.

I've seen people get wrapped up in making it a lot more complicated, myself included. Early in my career, Price Waterhouse Consulting had schooled me in its change methodology, presenting the same concepts in its own language. Change—the amount of resources on the topic can feel overwhelming. You might even experience a moment of panic, like I did, when searching on "Make Change Happen," to discover three billion websites. THREE BILLION. Where the heck do you begin? Cut through the noise and three questions emerge:

1. What do you want in the future?
2. What is your current reality today?
3. What actions will you take to move from your current reality to your desired future?

Framework upon framework, website upon website, share a version of these three questions. Many present highly validated and respected research that supports their approaches. Unfortunately, if you don't know this in the beginning, it can be easy to feel overwhelmed and find yourself swimming in an ocean of possibilities, thinking "What if . . . ?" Here's the deal; I'm practical. I'm not satisfied with "what ifs" that lead to "only ifs," and you shouldn't be, either.

The clearest framework that aligns with my thinking and simply explains why change initiatives succeed or fail is DVFR. For any change to occur, three elements must be present: Dissatisfaction with the current state, a Vision for the future, and a clear understanding of the First Steps to achieve the Vision. All must exist to overcome Resistance to Change: DVFR.[1] If you are missing D, V, or F, the likelihood that you will achieve the results you want is extremely low. From my personal experience, it just won't happen. In twenty years as an organizational change consultant, it is the most powerful change framework I've learned. I use it to launch Big Ideas and create New Realities.

Think of it as a *formula for change*: D x V x F > R. It's a metaphorical multiplication equation. As with any multiplication equation, if one element (D, V, or F) is zero, the product is zero. If you lack D, V, or F, then R will always be greater. Resistance to change is nearly impossible to overcome. Happy with your current state of affairs and lacking dissatisfaction? You won't launch your Big Idea. Feeling dissatisfied with your current situation but can't envision anything better? You won't create your New Reality. Clear on the vision of what you want to create and know why you are dissatisfied but don't have a clue on first steps to get started? You won't transform. Creating clarity with respect to these three primary elements creates a higher likelihood of success.

Recognizing a gap between what you want to create and what you are leaving behind is essential to inducing a need for change. No gap, nothing to do. DVFR could just as easily be VDFR. Whether you start by examining where you are or begin with a vision of what you would like to create does not matter. As long as you establish a gap between the two, Vision and Dissatisfaction, you can identify First Steps to close it and reach your destination. This book will support you in establishing and navigating the gap and identifying first steps by developing a compelling formula for your Big Idea or New Reality, however you choose to define it.

I want to let you in on a little secret I share with all of my clients. Somewhere on your journey, you will become so stuck that you will say, "Nope. No way. Not going forward. I'm done." I guarantee it will happen and, if you aren't careful, this thinking can create the *only if*. Many transformations fail because of it. It seems insurmountable when you don't know how to get past it. The uncertainty feels maddening. It is not surprising that many choose to escape it. Because it has been a powerful hurdle to overcome, I studied it with several teams. Interestingly, patience and wallowing in it actually create space to breakthrough. On average, four hours is all you need. Yes, seriously, four hours—by yourself, or with your team. Wallowing is not "I'm feeling stuck for fifteen minutes, so I'll take a break and come back to it." No. You must seriously immerse yourself and be stuck in place for a good four hours. When we reach this moment, I will remind you of this. You will remember it as a part of the experience and, hopefully, you will feel calmer and more confident because we predicted it. True. You'll see.

It's time to begin working with our formula, defining our DVFR or VDFR. I prefer the latter and will start with Vision.

TWO
VISION

Two days after returning from the Leading with Spirit retreat, my manager walked into my office and announced that there was a position opening in Madrid.

I jumped out of my chair screaming, "I knew it! I knew it! I knew this was going to happen!" The air felt electric as I told her about my vision of going to Spain. I immediately agreed to interview for the position the next week.

Unfortunately, two days after our conversation, Coke experienced a crisis in Belgium that changed the entire European business model. As a result, the job opportunity in Madrid suddenly disappeared. It had seemed like destiny and then—poof—vaporware. Confused and deflated, I wondered what this meant for my vision.

Two months later a different position surfaced. I was asked to interview to be the Chief of Staff to the president of Central Europe, based in Austria. Many people desired these roles. About thirty-five of them existed globally. They were a launch pad for "high potentials" and led to even greater roles of visibility and responsibility. I thought it was a long shot for me. In fact, when I was first asked to interview, I joked, "Why would I interview for that job? It always goes to a Marketing or Finance person. Why would they take an Org Change consultant?" In the end, three candidates made it to the final round: a person from Corporate Marketing, another from Corporate Finance, and me. Although I told my friends and family that my chances were slim, I believed deep down the job was mine. I didn't share my thinking because I feared jinxing it. Yet I could "see" myself in the job. A picture postcard floated in my mind—I was in the job in Austria. It was as if all I had to do to make it real was step into it. While I couldn't explain it, I believed the role was a part of my purpose in life. I was meant to go. I stopped thinking about Spain as I fixated on Austria.

When I walked off the plane in Vienna, I was exhausted. I hadn't slept due to anticipation and needed to shower and sleep before my afternoon interview. I was greeted by a driver who surprisingly explained that my interview had been rescheduled because the president had to travel in the afternoon. He asked, "Can you come to the office right now?"

My mind was a sleepless muddle, but, of course, I agreed.

During the interview, I remember being less than eloquent. I thought to myself, "What are you saying? Pull it together. You make no sense." But somehow, in the midst of my jet-lagged confusion, I must have made all of the right comments because, a couple of days later, Vienna called and offered me the job. It was late September.

Joe quit his job at Accenture, and by the middle of November we were living in Vienna. Later, I remembered Spain; it wasn't the right location or timing, but Austria was on the same continent. I was closer to my vision. Still, life sometimes throws curve balls. Within two weeks of arriving in Vienna, Coke's CEO resigned. The new CEO and my new boss were not allies; my boss was terminated. My job was tied to his and, just like that, my position was eliminated.

I panicked. What had I done? The sensible step would have been to return to Atlanta and try to get our old jobs back, but we still wanted to make Europe work. My friend Christy arranged an interview for me with her company in London. When I met the hiring manager, I asked about her sabbatical. Christy had mentioned it when she briefed me on the company and manager. She replied, "I walked El Camino de Santiago." Without understanding what it was, where it was located, or what it was about, my soul cried out, "I'm going to do that!"

Then, quite calmly, belying my excitement, I asked, "What is the Camino?" She described an eight hundred kilometer footpath across northern Spain that starts in the Pyrenees, along the border of France, and ends in Northwest Spain at Santiago de Compostela— the place believed to be the burial site of Saint James, one of Jesus's twelve disciples. El Camino de Santiago—the way of Saint James—is the pilgrimage to Santiago that began one thousand years ago and has been traveled by millions of individuals from all walks of life since.

It was February 2000, nine months after receiving "the call," and I finally understood my vision. I was going to walk El Camino de Santiago. This I knew, even though it seemed crazy to me.

LESSON TWO
Know Where You Are Going

At that moment, I had absolute clarity about my vision. I had experienced many spiritual mysteries or miracles in my life which couldn't be fully explained. However, I did not have faith in my physical abilities. I wasn't an athlete, a hiker, or a marine like my husband. My strength was emotional and spiritual but not physical. In a million years I would never have thought I could walk five miles, let alone five hundred. I tried a 10K once, and my knees killed me. Walking a medieval footpath on rocky trails seemed completely out of the question. Yet I was certain I would embark on this adventure that I didn't understand. I knew where I was going. I was going to Santiago, and the way there was El Camino. It was the only certain part of "the call." Like Caroll's famous character, Alice, I was falling down the rabbit hole. It was unclear to me how this would transpire, but walking to Santiago was as true to me as my perpetual love of dark chocolate.

Since then, I have come to understand that most people don't achieve the results they want for only two reasons:

1. They don't know what they want, and/or
2. They don't think they can have it.

It is that simple. When thinking of going to Santiago, I knew what I wanted, but I didn't think I could have it because I didn't feel capable. Who was I to go on this grand adventure?

When your vision isn't clear, you will start like Alice in Wonderland. If you want your New Reality to take root, a New Reality must be clear. You need to know what you really want. I've met so many people who are wandering aimlessly in life, bumping into opportunities that sometimes work and sometimes don't. When we know what we want in life, our actions can be much more prescriptive. Imagine the difference in planning a vacation when you say, "I want to see the volcanoes of Costa Rica," versus, "I'd like to go somewhere warm." *Clarity makes taking action easier.*

Of course, you might say, "I'm not even sure what I want to create. I want to change my situation, but what is my alternative?" Knowing what we want can be a daunting task. Some of us have followed the desires of those around us for so long that we have begun to confuse their desires with ours. Others have spent so much time listening to the inner voice of reason that we have abandoned our inner voice of desire.

Finally, many have turned power over to their *Inner Critic*, the internal voice pointing out every character flaw, inadequacy, and deficiency you fear to be true about yourself. The Inner Critic patiently weaves an intricate web of stories of past failures to prove the new endeavor will be futile. When you peel away the layers of stories the Inner Critic has told you about your limitations, it becomes obvious why you haven't thought you could achieve what it is you want. These powerful limiting beliefs prevent us from even dreaming about what we truly want. After all, why dream if you know you can't have it? However, when you get right down to it, what's the harm of wanting something just for the sheer delight of wanting it?

Say you have finally given yourself permission *to want*, what do you choose? How do you discover it? As I observed in my Camino experience, I have had moments of clarity in which knowing what I wanted became so powerful that it became a guiding force in my life. However, like everyone, I've also had moments when I didn't have a clue; I only knew the current situation was intolerable. Fortunately, when stuck, you have some questions to help you to both discover a vision and frame it to be as productive as possible.

First, ask yourself this simple, open-ended question: "What do I want?" Then, actually give yourself a moment to reflect before answering it. You might be surprised. Often, a quick yet unexpected response emerges, if you allow it to. When a question is posed, a unique set of events occurs in the brain. Often, just asking the question enables the answer to surface.[2] If you don't get an answer right away, focus your attention elsewhere. The answer may come when you least expect it. People often have answers pop into their heads when they are in the shower, go for a walk, or when they just wake up. If you don't receive an answer, Chapter Two of Part Two provides exercises to explore this further.

It is also important to create the environment and energy for your vision to thrive. Mindset and framing, rooted in neuroscience and physics, are the foundation of vision.

Mindset is a way of thinking, an attitude or belief about how you see the world, life, work, etc. Is the glass half-empty or half-full? You might think your mindset is just a part of who you are and not possible to change. You think you are a half-empty kind of girl, and so you are. But you don't have to be. Mindset is changeable and flexible. In her book, *Mindset*, Dr. Carol Dweck describes two primary mindsets: *fixed* and *growth*. Fixed proposes your qualities are carved in stone and creates an urgency to prove yourself over and over. Growth asserts your basic qualities can be developed through your efforts. You can evolve through application and experience."[3] In infancy, you don't know the difference; most likely you think you can have all that you want or need. So, how does the fixed mindset develop? Well-meaning but anxious parenting might have something to do with it. Corrections like "Don't touch the hot stove," "Don't run into the street," and "Don't climb your dresser" suggest the world is filled with danger and limitations. To have a vision, choose the half-full, anything is possible, growth mindset.

Framing follows mindset. Framing is a mindset's language. Is your vision framed in the negative or the positive? From the laws of physics, we know the concept of the path of least resistance. It describes the physical or metaphorical pathway that provides the least resistance to forward motion by a given object or entity, among a set of alternative paths.[4] Oooh, that's a mouthful. Simply stated, energy goes where it is easiest for it to go. Water flows downhill; cow-paths were created by lazy cows choosing the easiest ways to cross hills. How does this apply to vision? Focus on what you *want* and move toward that. You'd be surprised how many people I work with tell me their goals by telling me what they DON'T want: "I don't want to lose my job," "I don't want to be a bookkeeper anymore," or "I don't want to feel so lethargic." It's a stream of "I don't want . . .

I don't want . . . I don't want . . ." The terrible irony is that each time they utter what they don't want, their brain focuses on that precise concern.

Let me explain. Don't think of a red car. What happens? Of course, you think of a red car. But do you know why you think of a red car? Your brain does not understand a negative in the absence of the positive. Or, more precisely, as soon as you read, "Don't think of a red car," your brain MUST think of a red car to understand what it shouldn't think of.[5] Instead, it would be better to read, "Think of a blue cow" or "Think of a pink elephant." The red car would not enter the picture, and you would never think of it.

Sounds too simple? Feeling a little skeptical? Have you ever observed a parent say to a child, "Don't spill your milk," just to watch the glass, seconds later, topple over, with the milk running down the table and onto the floor? Ahh, the young brain at work; it saw "spill the milk" first and responded accordingly. Say, "Hold onto your milk," and watch for better results.

When the economy declines, have you ever thought, "I don't want to lose my job"? First, the brain focuses on *lose my job*. Hmmm, probably not the best idea to emphasize. When we create vision, instead we focus on what we DO want: "I want to keep my job," "I want to work with children," "I want to have energy," or "I want to change the world!" Bottom line, frame your vision in the positive.

After greater clarity of the Vision from the DVFR/VDFR formula, it's time to explore Dissatisfaction. Let's next take a look at what is happening in your current situation.

THREE
DISSATISFACTION

In spite of the revelation about the meaning of my vision, I still had the impending loss of my job in Vienna and myriad complications associated with it to resolve first. After completing our interviews in London, Joe and I returned to Vienna realizing we didn't want to move there. Instead, we wanted to live in Spain. Joe is half Spanish and bilingual. We refocused our job search on Madrid, where Joe had friends.

As the job search in Madrid ensued, I helped in the downsizing of Coke's Central European organization. The Vienna office alone experienced a ninety percent reduction in force, or RIF. Coke's hiring of an Org Change consultant had been oddly prescient in the cosmic scheme of life. A chief of staff with a Marketing or Finance background would have been less equipped to assist with the magnitude of organizational change. Synchronicity. I was exactly where I was meant to be in order to help people in a time of need and to see the impact of restructuring from an acutely intimate perspective. It was humbling. This wasn't just business—this was personal, terribly personal.

Being a part of the downsizing was demanding and emotionally draining. In the end, and as expected, my job was also eliminated. Fortunately, Joe was hired by a consulting firm in Madrid, and eight months after arriving in Vienna, we found ourselves moving countries once more. We left Austria in mid-July 2000, with our one car stuffed so high in the back seat that our two dogs, sitting on dog beds atop our belongings, could easily see out the windows as we drove.

Joe wasn't due in Madrid until September, so we made a vacation of it. We took our time driving to Madrid via Italy and France, and even drove to southern Spain to spend time with some of Joe's family who lived there. During this time, I made a decision. I would take time off and stop looking for a job for six months.

It was a big moment for me. Starting with a paper route at nine years, I had worked out of necessity throughout my youth as a babysitter, house cleaner, golf course attendant, fast food cashier, etc. For much of my childhood, I lived in a single-parent home under the poverty line. I bought my clothes and school supplies. If I wanted to be involved in school activities, I was responsible for paying for them. I worked three jobs to pay expenses during college. After college, I worked like a fiend to be given incredible opportunities in my career, like the one in Vienna. Moving to Europe was, in many respects, like winning the lottery. So, taking time off was an unheard-of luxury. It turned out to be a blessing, because we had nearly sixty visitors in our first nine months of living in Madrid.

While I guided our guests through Spain and learned Spanish, Joe began his new role as a director at a large multinational consulting firm. By January 2001, it was clear that the job wasn't what he had expected. In fact, my husband, the marine reservist, whom I jokingly told people was so tough that he could sleep in the dirt and eat it, a man who never complained, was miserable. He left the consulting firm and accepted a position at a new European office of a US-based executive search firm with whom he had a prior relationship. The job was one hundred percent commission. I was nervous about our financial security, but a severance package provided by Coke created a cushion that allowed us time while the search firm launched in Europe and he could earn his first commission.

For the first three months in the new job, he traveled and built relationships with organizations but did not earn any money. We had expected this, because it normally took three months in the United

States to see a return on investment. We thought it might take a few more months in Europe. While we were waiting for the return to materialize, we learned I was pregnant. We were thrilled about the pregnancy, yet nervous about the lack of income to support ourselves and the baby. Instead of giving up, we decided that Joe would take a three-month Marine Corps Reserve assignment at Camp Lejeune in the United States. He could manage his new business relationships remotely during that time, and it would provide regular income plus more time to figure out our next step—stay in Europe with the new job or return to the United States and find employment there.

Joe left for Camp Lejeune in mid-June 2001, right after I had completed my first trimester. He would be gone during my second trimester, but we weren't concerned since we knew I had already passed the first.

The day he left, I had a doctor's appointment scheduled. While Joe was enroute to the United States, the doctor said in Spanish, "Shannon, I'm very sorry. I can't find the heartbeat." Because my Spanish was not perfect, I hoped that I had misunderstood. I hadn't. I learned that I had miscarried three weeks earlier in what is referred to as a "missed miscarriage," a rare and cruel trick of the body.

I was devastated and felt terribly alone as the doctor described the procedure and hospital stay required. I had no way of immediately contacting Joe, which added to my feeling of isolation. By the time I could talk to him, I was so overcome by emotion from the situation, I found it difficult to share the dreadful news.

The remainder of the summer was painful, but as mid-September approached, I looked forward to Joe's return. When 9/11 happened. Joe was still on active duty. As a communications officer, he was mobilized to Stuttgart, Germany, where the satellite systems are monitored. Our decision to stay or go was on hold.

Fortunately, he was given a few days of leave (vacation to us civilians) to stop off at home in Madrid before moving to his assignment in Stuttgart, and I was blessed to become pregnant again. We were thrilled. Even though Joe wasn't present, I looked forward to our future family, and my doctor seemed quite certain I would be fine. He assured me a second miscarriage was unlikely and approved my travel to Houston for the birth of my sister's first child. Because of my history, he recommended I continue my regular doctor's visits and see an obstetrician while I was in the United States. He assured me that he didn't expect any complications.

When I arrived, my sister delivered her baby, and the next day I went to her doctor. To my shock and disappointment, I discovered I had miscarried again. During this challenging time, I was grateful to have the support of my sister, but it was bittersweet with a new nephew at home.

I returned to Madrid and traveled to Stuttgart to see Joe over the holidays. On New Year's Eve, as we toasted the New Year, Joe said solemnly, "Shannon, it was a tough year, but it's over and it can't get any worse." Immediately, my stomach turned over and I thought, "Oh no, something really bad is coming."

A few days later, my mother called and told me she had cancer. My first thought was, "No way, this can't be happening. I've lost my job, my husband is mobilized, I've had two miscarriages, and now my mother has cancer." My mother is my rock. Through the many tough times my family experienced, she hung in there. I started to cry, and she said, "Don't worry, the doctor says it isn't that bad. It's only Stage 1. She's scheduled surgery in four weeks."

I flew to the United States to help my mother recover from her surgery. We didn't expect her to need chemotherapy or radiation, but we knew that she would be off her feet for a few weeks. Surgery revealed a much more serious case of Stage 4 cancer which had metastasized to her lymph nodes and rib cage. A short surgical recovery turned into months of chemotherapy and radiation. When most of the treatments were completed in May, I returned home, emotionally and physically exhausted. With Joe still in Stuttgart, and unsure of my next move, I started to read the many books I had collected about the Camino.

Shortly after my return, Joe was able to take leave. When he arrived home, he noticed the pile of books on my side of the bed. He looked at the books, then at me, and asked, "Are you going to walk the Camino now?" I stared at him, paralyzed, as the following thoughts went through my head in a millisecond, "Why am I reading *these books? Am I going to walk the Camino? How can I go at this time? We've been separated for nearly a year? It's been a terrible year. We should be together now. We should be starting our family." While I stared at him like a deer-in-the-headlights, he said, "I want you to go."*

LESSON THREE
Know What You Are Leaving Behind

Prior to walking the Camino, my situation had become so intolerable that it should have been obvious that I should do something—anything—different. But sometimes we are pushed beyond our breaking point. Like the frog slowly boiled to death after first being placed in a pot of cold water, I had come to tolerate my lot in life. After the loss, pain, and fear of the prior year and a half, I felt so beaten that I didn't think my life would, or could, be different. I expected the worst to happen. Consumed by all that was wrong with my world, I had become a glass-half-empty kind of girl!

Dissatisfaction, the *D* in the DVFR model, was something that I had in spades. But dissatisfaction has a sweet spot. Too much, and it consumes you; too little, and there's no reason to change. Why is dissatisfaction so important to the process of creating a New Reality? Nothing will change without dissatisfaction. Zero. Nada. Nothing. This idea of needing dissatisfaction might sound daunting, especially after you heard not only dissatisfaction but also despair in my story. I mean, why would anyone want that? Who, in their right mind, wants to feel dissatisfaction, let alone despair? There is more to the answer than simply whether or not we're comfortable with the concept of dissatisfaction. Dissatisfaction has many dimensions and levels, from frustration to despair. Do you need to feel completely hopeless? No. Must you feel frustrated, irritated, annoyed? Most likely. The DVFR model does not claim one element as more important than another. It's like a braid with the three strands of D, V, and F woven together, enabling us to overcome the power of inertia.

Inertia? This takes us back to basic physics. You probably learned this in middle school and forgot it after the test. Newton's first law of motion states a body at rest remains at rest, while a body in motion remains in motion, unless an externally applied force acts on it. Similarly, human beings and organizations do not change unless an external force propels them in a new direction. To change, a force must oppose the inertia, but the inertia will resist the force. For human beings and organizations, the interwoven braid of Dissatisfaction, Vision, and First Steps is the force. Lose one of the strands in the braid, and the force is gone. My story exemplifies the simple truth that clarity of vision isn't enough and doesn't provide any guarantee that we'll take action to create a New Reality.

Dissatisfaction must be present and plays an integral role in enabling you to move toward your New Reality. Wonder why you are happy to sit on your bed and binge-watch shows, instead of getting in motion to make a happier and healthy body? You might be dissatisfied with your current state of being, but most likely, you are not dissatisfied enough. Or, you might be racked with despair over the losses in your life and paralyzed in your bed, for which circumstance Netflix is a wonderful escape.

Where does this leave us? Too little, we are inert. Too much, we are paralyzed by our agony. Must we wait for our circumstances to gradually worsen until we reach a tipping point where we have so much gut-wrenching pain that we have no choice but to take action? Do we have another way beyond disaster to create D (Dissatisfaction) versus d (disillusionment)? How do we find the sweet spot of dissatisfaction that propels us forward?

The sweet spot might be in a different place than where you have been looking. Based on years of personal and observed experience, I've noticed it is fairly easy to wallow in disillusionment or mild dissatisfaction for long periods of time, and this just won't cut it. Try this exercise: Think of a goal you have wanted to accomplish but haven't. What is your level of dissatisfaction? How long has this particular dissatisfaction been present? If it has been present for a while and/or you view it as an ever-present obstacle or pattern of behavior that you never seem to overcome, most likely, you haven't really dug deep enough. You have to be much like a miner, chiseling through the cave rock, seeking the gold, the D. In some cases, you may actually have to blast the cave to find it.

When I started writing this book, much in my life was going well. I didn't have the dissatisfaction. I had a loving family. My career satisfied me. Writing a book wasn't necessary and seemed like a lot of work. Yet it nagged at the back of my brain, asking to be written. Unlike my days before the Camino, dissatisfaction was lacking. The only concern I could tap into was the idea that the book didn't exist. I didn't have the D. Determined to find it, I asked myself a simple question that I ask all of my coaching clients, "What is getting in the way of achieving your goal?"

The most obvious answer, time. I'm always overcommitted. ALWAYS. So, how can I possibly add one more activity? Yet as I always tell my clients, "Time is an illusion." And I firmly believe it. We all have moments when time seems to slow down, even stand still, as if we are observing all events happening in slow motion from outside of our bodies. We also have experiences when it goes by so fast that we have no idea what happened to the day.

Time was not my problem. How I chose to prioritize and manage my time was my problem. If I wanted to write a book, I would have to prioritize differently. I wondered if I could eliminate an activity. I inventoried my time. I discovered that I spent an inordinate amount of it, forty-five minutes per morning, tidying my messy kitchen—putting away mail and bills that covered the kitchen table, rinsing and recycling items (I'm a dedicated recycler), sweeping the floor where crumbs had accumulated. The mess distracted me to the point that I couldn't focus.

The irony was staggering because I actually thrive in a messy office. I am a creative. I have multiple projects started. I have piles of paper, know exactly what is in each pile and can find any paper I need. What the heck was different about the kitchen? And why was I spending forty-five minutes a day, five days of the week, but NOT on the weekend, cleaning it? If I could get rid of this one task, I could free up nearly four hours of time each week.

After some journaling on the topic, I discovered . . .

I clean my kitchen because *I fear what YOU might think of me.* My kitchen is at the front of my house and surrounded by floor-to-ceiling windows. You might walk by or enter my home and see it. Then, you might think I am incredibly disorganized, even incompetent. Worse, you will tell others, "It is a ruse. It is an illusion. She doesn't have it all together. She is not Superwoman. If she is that disorganized, she can't be that competent. We shouldn't listen to ANYTHING she has to say." And then you will not hire me. And then I won't have a business. And then I won't be able to support my family. And then . . . And then . . . And then . . . As you can see, it's a vicious downward spiral. Instead of risking your bad opinion of me, *I clean up the darn kitchen to look good for you!*

I, not YOU, choose to buy into the crap I tell myself on my worst days. I, not YOU, choose to clean my kitchen instead of writing a book that I believe in my heart is much more meaningful than straightening up my kitchen. Do

I have *D*-as-in-Dissatisfaction now? You better believe it! I'm done, *D*-as-in-Dissatisfaction done, with living in fear about what you think of me. It doesn't serve me or you. I have a book to write, and the book can help both of us. If I can reveal and live with my truth, maybe you can, too, and maybe the world will be a much better place because of it. Don't wait for your partner to lose his job or for someone you love to get sick. If you came to this book with a great idea but lacking dissatisfaction, we'll work together to make you just dissatisfied enough for you to take action. In the workbook, we'll mine for some reasonable and compelling dissatisfaction. So, let's raise our glasses . . . and chocolates . . . to the metaphorical messy kitchens, which support Big Ideas, New Realities, and books waiting to be written.

FOUR
FIRST STEPS

When Joe said, "I want you to go," the last tumbler fell into place. Until that moment, the Camino was merely a mystical vision, a fantasy about a journey I couldn't truly imagine completing because I had never done anything remotely like it before and certainly didn't think I was capable. If I was to walk the Camino, then magic would have to transform me into a person who could walk across Spain. I couldn't imagine anything that magical happening to me.

Now, after the loss, pain, and fear that I had experienced throughout the prior year and a half, I had begun living with an expectation of the worst happening, and I couldn't shake that feeling. I didn't want to think that way, but I thought along that line anyway. I wanted to put the pain behind me, but I didn't know how. I was numb and believed nothing positive was going to happen to me ever again. And as a coach, as someone with a degree in human development, I knew something was terribly wrong. I knew I needed to let go of some of my current ways in order to move forward in my life. When Joe said I should go, his words confirmed to me that he knew it too. It wasn't my imagination. It was real, and I wasn't hiding it from anyone. At the same time, I felt scared because I wondered if something in me had broken forever. If there was a solution, it was in something beyond myself. How the Camino could help me through this season wasn't clear, but I felt certain it *offered a better option than what plagued me at that point in time. And so, my decision was made; my Camino had started.*

As his words sank in and my deer-in-the-headlights moment passed, I remembered my friend Susan, who lived in Washington, DC. The thought startled me because it came immediately after I made my decision, as if it had been waiting for the moment. Susan was one of my closest friends from graduate school and had visited us shortly after we moved to Madrid. She had studied in Spain during college. When she visited Spain, I told her about my vision of walking the Camino. Susan had studied in Santiago and had seen the pilgrims on their way to the cathedral. She replied, "When you go, let me know; I'd like to go too." I promised to contact her when I was ready.

Still, I hesitated. Susan had started a new job three months earlier, and I doubted that she could come. But I couldn't stop thinking about her. Her words continued to echo through my mind and told me to reach out to her. Although it didn't make logical sense to me, I knew I would regret it if I didn't contact her. I sent her an email with two sentences. "I am leaving for the Camino in two weeks. Do you want to join me?" The next day, I opened my laptop to read, "Funny you should ask, I just lost my job. I'm coming."

LESSON FOUR
Engage Your Supporters

I don't believe in coincidence. I do believe in synchronicity, and I certainly believe in miracles of all shapes and sizes. I view Susan's availability as a small miracle, a predesigned shift in her life force energy to support mine, as well as her life's journey. In that moment, Susan and I had a shared purpose, entwined in a way that we couldn't fully explain, and yet designed before either of us ever stepped foot on the Camino. Susan's calling had come years before mine, but required an unexpected loss of a job and an invitation from a girlfriend to be activated. Mine required lessons in pain and loss of a different nature and, finally, an invitation from my husband to step forward. Our paths joined in that moment to create a wonderful New Reality for ourselves. Susan was an integral part of my Camino experience, and I will always have a special bond with her because she accepted my invitation.

Early in my consulting career, I learned that once you have created your vision and have analyzed your current state (recognizing dissatisfaction), the gap becomes visible. That's when it's time to consider who has a stake in the outcome. Fittingly, these people are called our stakeholders, and I **always** start with them. In good change management approaches, analyzing your various stakeholder populations and why they support or oppose your project is critical to ensuring it is implemented. I call these individuals "Supporters" or "Opposers."

Identifying and engaging your Supporters early in the process improves your chance of success. Supporters are the stakeholders who enthusiastically embrace the change and are willing to advocate on your behalf. For example, Joe and Susan were my Supporters. Opposers don't embrace the change and actively work to block your success. We all have both groups in our lives. If an Opposer carries a lot of influence and power in your life, they can quickly derail you. Joe could have been an Opposer as easily as a Supporter, and he is an eminently important stakeholder in my world. If he had said, "Are you going to walk the Camino now? Why would you do that when I just returned home? I really want to be with you," instead of, "I want you to go," I doubt I'd be sharing this story now. Susan was a different type of stakeholder. While she was a Supporter who had expressed a high level of interest in the Camino in the past, she held less influence in my life. I would have still gone, even if she had chosen not to join me. At the beginning of my journey, Susan's role seemed complementary, but not critical, to completing my trip.

I have learned in the years since then that, any time I find myself stuck, the first step I must take is to look for support. It isn't natural for me to do. As a firstborn child in a dysfunctional family, I took on the role of "hero-child." Firstborns tend to be self-assured, high achievers, driven, with a lot of confidence. Firstborns aren't the sole heirs to this archetype, nor are all firstborns bound to it, but many often possess it. In families with extraordinary stress and dysfunction, the roles can become exaggerated.

I didn't just achieve, I super-achieved. Everything I did was an exaggeration, a caricature of what might be called typical. In my family environment, I learned to rely solely on myself. Others could ALWAYS count on me when I said I'd be there for them, but it NEVER occurred to me to ask for help. I didn't expect it, and, if someone offered it, I would decline. I felt incredibly uncomfortable accepting help. I thought my job was to solve the world's problems. No task was too big for this "hero-child." It's hardly surprising that I dug myself into such a pit of despair prior to the Camino. It never occurred to me to let anyone know just how much I was suffering.

I observe this pattern in many of my female clients. Many women haven't been taught to ask for help or reach out. Part of this stems from our mothers and grandmothers. As they started entering the work environment in the second half of the twentieth century, their primary jobs at home did not go away. The message they received was, "Go ahead and get a job in the world of work, but don't forget your primary job is at home." Meanwhile, their husbands kept doing their jobs in the world of work, but usually didn't assume any new responsibilities at home. My generation observed this behavior and didn't fully question it until we started to rise into roles of much greater responsibility at work. This led to some passionate conversations/arguments, helping men to understand the necessity of helping maintain a home and raise a family. While I am grateful to see some shifts in these trends happening in my own life and in the lives of my own daughters and nieces, I fear it is changing too slowly. Because our world has become increasingly complex and challenging over time, achieving success is also more demanding. Stubborn and absolute self-reliance sets a person up for failure. To create a New Reality, you must have support, reach out, and ask for help.

In a synchronistic moment, Susan was able to join me because I remembered our conversation and invited her and she was interested, willing, and available. If I hadn't invited her, my Camino experience would have been different. Susan turned out to be essential to my success! Would I have made it to Santiago if she had not been there to encourage me or act as my accountability buddy? How easy would it have been to stop if I didn't have a partner who reminded me each day of our next stop along the Camino.

To find your Supporters, tell your friends and colleagues about the New Reality you want to create. Invite their input. Tell them you want a different career, a healthier lifestyle, to run a marathon, to launch a non-profit to eradicate poverty in the world, or write a book! Pay close attention to who shows interest and support for whatever IT is. You are less likely to back out when someone not only encourages you but also agrees to accompany you on your journey. Furthermore, your Supporters may have hidden talents or connections that will help you arrive at your destination, so your probability of success increases. Ultimately, to *WE the Change*, invite your Supporters to join you—they might just surprise you.

FIVE
THE RIGHT GEAR

In the time period that I waited for Susan to arrive, I began to pack. I consulted with a friend of a friend who had walked the Camino in the past. The backpack goal? No more than twenty pounds. It may sound like a lot, but when I included the weight of the backpack, water, and bad-weather gear, I had to be thoughtful about each article I would be carrying. I deliberated over each item. Clothespin or safety pin? Safety pin—smaller and more versatile. Journal or book? Journal— better to capture my own thoughts than to read someone else's. Flip flops or hiking sandals? Flip flops—lighter, dry faster.

Two weeks later, Susan arrived in Madrid. Given her desire to search for a job and mine to be with Joe after our lengthy separation, we had decided that we would only walk for about two weeks, or about half the route. Many pilgrims—the term used for those who walk the Camino—walk the length of the Camino a week at a time. They start in one place, walk for a week, and return the following year, picking up where they left off. We had the same plan. We had our packs and walking sticks—everything we believed we needed for our journey.

The following morning, before the break of dawn, we were on a train taking us to Pamplona, the closest city to Roncesvalles we could get to by train. Roncesvalles is the town on the Spanish border with France where the Camino originates. We arrived around ten in the morning to discover that the bus to Roncesvalles did not leave until much later in the afternoon.

We were much too excited to wait for the bus. Realizing it was only forty-four kilometers (twenty-seven miles) east to Roncesvalles and being girls from the city, we hailed a taxi. Ironically, we traveled east to Roncesvalles so we could walk west and pass through Pamplona a few days later.

Winding through the mountain switchbacks was more time-consuming than I had expected. A shocking revelation hit me. Thinking out loud, I blurted, "It's a long way to Pamplona."

Susan replied, "You're just getting that?"

What I meant was, "What was I thinking? The cab ride is taking forever and **first we have to walk back to Pamplona**. Am I kidding myself? I'm going to walk to Pamplona with twenty pounds on my back? I'm not an athlete. I haven't prepared." I could feel panic rising like bile. I thought of quitting, but pride stopped me.

We arrived in Roncesvalles to discover that the Pilgrim Center at the church was closed. At the Center, we intended to collect our

Pilgrim's Passports—documents pilgrims carry which serve as proof of the journey. When they arrive in Santiago, pilgrims use it to request the Compostela, the official document commemorating completion of the Camino. In addition, passports are required to obtain lodging at refugios—refuge places with beds, showers, and kitchens for pilgrims. A refugio is the rustic equivalent of a dormitory. It provides the basics. Hot water is a bonus. As pilgrims walk the Camino each day, they search for shelter for the night in a refugio. Each refugio stamps the passport with its unique seal, creating a record and memento of the journey.

As we waited for the Center to open, we talked to other peregrinos (pilgrims). We met two Canadians, Christine and Judy. For some reason—maybe I watched too many movies with Canadian Mounties as a kid—I believe that all Canadians are outdoorsy and avid hikers. These two matched that image to perfection with packs twice the size of ours and containing the latest and greatest hiking gear. As they inventoried their gear and demonstrated the best way to buckle a pack around the hips, they seemed so knowledgeable. Even after reading six books about the Camino and doing my research, my doubts were piling up. I could feel my anxiety in the pit of my stomach; I wondered if we were truly ready for the Camino.

LESSON FIVE
Pack Light

Self-doubt stops more journeys before they begin, before the first step is even taken, so people never get to their destinations or launch their Big Ideas or create their New Realities. I am no exception. Still, some people do make it. How does it happen? Are they superior to us in some way? I don't think so. Starting any journey can be overwhelming. Even when I go on vacation and am really excited, I can feel it, especially if I am traveling internationally with my family. I fear we will have a minor medical incident, such as an intestinal virus from bad drinking water, and we won't be able to get any help, so I overpack with items and medicines like Pepto-Bismol which are rarely used. I plan for it even when

I know, having lived in both Austria and Spain, that it is easier to directly purchase the medical supplies or prescription medicines I need when I'm in Europe than when I'm in the U.S. But for me, a part of being a mother is being prepared . . . for any challenge . . . for any disaster. I learned it from my mom, whose Mary Poppins-like purse carried all necessary tools for any occasion. Scissors, glue, sewing kit, Band-Aids, pocket dictionary? She had them. Apparently, one never knows when clothing, humans, or English homework might need repair.

I came to believe that mothers should be prepared for all possibilities at all times. And I assume that I won't be able to get what I need in a foreign country. Thus, I overpack. In my profession, these beliefs and assumptions are called *mental models*, frameworks of how we think the world works, even how the world-of-work, works. Frameworks guide our behavior, though we often aren't aware of them until they are challenged. They have two primary benefits. With them, life is a little easier and a little safer. Imagine if you had to relearn how to cross the street at a traffic intersection every day. Fortunately, green means go, and red means stop to many people in the world. Frameworks and models order the would-be chaos of our world.

Mental models can have drawbacks. When I became focused on my belief that I am naive about what would be required to walk the Camino—strength, athleticism, knowledge about hiking, my bad luck at not being born Canadian— my mind churned in a mental model that expertise is required. It was a bad story that could have stopped me in my tracks before I ever stepped onto the Camino. Stories like these stop our journeys. Mental models can support or derail us.

Why didn't I start with a better, more positive story? I have certainly overcome plenty of obstacles in my life. I have proven I am capable. Still, put me in a new situation and I don't start with the mantra, "I am capable. All is well. I've got this." Where is Glenda the Good Witch when we need her to encourage us with "You are capable of more than you know . . . You had the power all along, my dear." Instead, W3, the Wicked Witch of the West, hisses in my ear, "I'll get you, my pretty. You aren't ready. You don't have a clue. What are you doing? Who are you to take on this big task?" Fortunately, my DVFR for the Camino was compelling and a different, smaller, and quieter voice called, "But then, who are you not to go? If not you, then who? If not now, then when?"

Around this same time, I worked with a coach. She asked what I believed it was that helped me to be successful. I commented that it was a lot of hard work. She wondered if that had always been true. I said, "Yes, I think so." She persisted, "Is that true for everyone?" I started to laugh and explained that I had always thought that all feats were easy for Joe. Life always just worked out for him. Sometimes it really pissed me off. Next, my coach suggested, "Could it be easy for you too?" "No," was my quick reply. "Are you sure about that?" she responded. "Yes, pretty sure." She asked me to try on the belief that things could be easy. I attempted to adopt it as my own, but it felt so physically uncomfortable, so false to me, I literally shivered. Intellectually, I understood her desire to help me break though my belief that everything worthwhile required hard work, but emotionally I couldn't do it.

Then she asked me a simple yet brilliant question, "Could it be easier?" Her slight turn of phrase created a new possibility, stopped my whirling brain, and made me think. She continued, "Are there ways to accomplish your goals that you have never considered, may not even know about, that could make it easier?" Her questions caught me completely by surprise. She asked me to try this new idea on: *It could be easier.* This time it fit. It seemed true for me. Yes, it could be easier. After working with her, I constructed goals differently. I'd express my goal and include the easier mantra to support and reinforce it: "I want to achieve Goal A and to discover an easier way to achieve it." Since then, I have discovered simple and sometimes effortless techniques to accomplish my goals. Now I say, "I want to achieve Goal B and for it to be easy." Interestingly, I've noticed that what I consider easy might be hard for my clients and vice versa. I've learned what's "easy" is relative.

To reveal our mental models, we have to ask ourselves new questions, just as my coach asked me. What do you believe to be true about how you achieve success in the world? What if you are wrong? What becomes possible for you if you let go of these beliefs? Have you ever been completely certain about an idea only to discover you were absolutely wrong? Why were you wrong? How did you discover your error? Don't stop there. Challenge your assumptions before believing they are true.

Ultimately, we carry more than backpacks and hand luggage on our journeys. We carry the baggage of mental models, beliefs, and assumptions, that can either encourage or discourage our forward movement. To create our New Reality, we will have to learn to let go of the internal stories that impede our progress. We'll have to pack light.

SIX
DECISIONS

Attempting to distract myself from my certainty that I was both ill-prepared and ill-equipped for the Camino while I waited for the Pilgrim Center to open, I turned my attention to the church. Built in the thirteenth century's early Gothic style, it is a beautiful work of artistic architecture. It was easy to distract myself with the details. Connected to it stood the refugio, the first and largest I would experience. It had been built in 1127 to provide a hospital for pilgrims along the Camino. It was staggering to contemplate the number of souls who had entered its halls and found refuge within it during the past 800 years. Soon, I would be one of them.

When the Center opened, I requested my passport and made my way to my first refugio. I checked in with the hospitalero, or host of the refugio, and received my first Camino stamp for my passport. As I entered, I was filled with the "buzz" of energy left behind by the pilgrims who had traveled before me. The energy and spirit of the place was intoxicating and left me with the sense that this wasn't my first time to walk the Camino. I felt as if I had stepped back in history and was about to engage in a long-understood and agreed-upon rite of passage. This was juxtaposed with what would become our daily ritual for the remainder of our journey. Susan and I found a bed, unpacked, showered, and then searched for dinner. Unlike the days *to follow, we did not need to wash our clothes. In most refugios, pilgrims cook their meals with others. In Roncesvalles—the starting place—pilgrims dine together in a small café.*

From the moment we began to unpack in our room of thirty tightly crowded bunk beds, the questions began. "Where are you from?" asked one voice. "Are you going to Santiago?" called another. As I noted earlier, Susan and I didn't plan to go to Santiago. We were going as far as we could in the next two weeks. As the other pilgrims asked me, "Are you going to Santiago?" I felt an uncomfortable and uncontrollable response rumbling from deep in my heart, as it had done when I first heard of the Camino. "Yes!" it shouted, "I am going to Santiago!" But my head was more rational, "No, that wasn't the agreement. I told Joe I am only walking for two weeks." He was briefly home for leave; I couldn't be gone for a month. Besides, Susan had to get back to start her job search and we were now in this together.

However, the next morning Susan said to me, "I just want you to know that I've decided to go to Santiago." I responded, "Me, too!" In a flash, we committed to a more specific destination. It was no longer just about the Camino—it was about getting to Santiago!

LESSON SIX
Commit to Going and Go!

As I decided to go to Santiago, I was effectively deciding to not spend as much time with Joe, and I had a mild pang of guilt. I had to tell him and felt uncomfortable about it. I believed he'd support me, but I felt selfish and didn't like the feeling. I also had lingering self-doubt. I had not actually walked one step on the path of Santiago at this point. I certainly looked the part of the pilgrim with my gear. I had had enough commitment to invite a friend, take a train to Pamplona, hail a taxi to Roncesvalles, and find a bed in my first refugio. BUT, I was simultaneously facing the unknown as well as many unwelcome beliefs about how unworthy and incapable I was to execute my plan. I didn't know what I didn't know; and so, I was anxious. Plus, I wanted to spend time with my husband.

I had all of the right conditions to rationalize abandoning my commitment and not walking the full distance. I was stuck in what my profession calls *the neutral zone*, or what others might call limbo or sitting on the fence. It's an odd place because you have kicked off the project, realized you don't know everything you need to know, and have a sense the work is greater than you expected. At this point on the Camino, I knew enough to get to the starting line but I didn't think I knew enough to finish. I could only imagine what might be required to do so.

Waffling back and forth is normal at this stage of launching the Big Idea or creating a New Reality. The distance seems too far; the work required to get there, too great. On the surface, wondering whether to stay or go seems rational. Yet as we have discovered, much is happening beneath the surface. The waters are murky with lingering self-doubt: *Have I made the right decision?* Rational thought amplifies the doubt: "My decision isn't sound. I don't know what I'm doing, I'm not an expert, I have no right to make this decision. What alternative possibilities/choices am I saying no to if I pursue this idea? I could spend more time with my family. I could pursue other interests." Still, staying stuck is a decision to do nothing. Harsh but true. Even if it doesn't seem quite as obvious, it is as much of a decision as choosing to move forward.

Similarly, as I worked on my current Big Idea, this book, I had a comparable experience to that moment on the Camino. I wondered, *Do I want to finish writing this book?* I was plagued with doubts, such as: "It requires discipline. It takes me away from my family. I don't know how long it might take. It seems more overwhelming than I thought it would. Can I actually finish it?"

In a burst of insight, I suddenly recognized my place on the path and felt a wave of disbelief. *What? I'm on the fence?! Seriously? So soon?* I felt betrayed by my own mind! My knowledge and experience could not protect me from my doubts. If I, an individual who not only walked the Camino but also started many new ventures in my career, could find myself unconsciously succumbing to my doubts, what could I possibly expect of my clients who are venturing into this space, possibly for the first time?

I felt momentarily dizzy and dismayed, until I remembered my Critic's Journal. My coach, Marcia Zina Mager, gave me this tool to use when my self-talk is highly negative. I have also found it helpful when I'm only mildly confused. The Critic's Journal allows time to pause, reflect, and become aware of what is happening in mind and body. It helps to express thinking and feelings, positive or negative. When I use it, I become calmer and more clear-minded. As this happens, I am able to create space to focus and move forward. The writing tends to be cathartic. Once I have physically written the tornado of thoughts swirling in my head and have released the negativity, I often find solutions for what is perplexing me.

In my Critic's Journal, I contemplated whether or not to continue writing the book. I wrote and wrote and wrote, and then, I laughed at myself. I discovered, *Of course, I'm on the fence. I am exactly where I am supposed to be at this point.* I told you we would hit a place where we think we can't move forward. This is that place. And it won't be the only time.

As I continued to reflect, I thought of when I first started speaking about my experience along the Camino. People would say to me, "You should write a book." My ego was flattered, and I'd think to myself, as a queen on her throne speaking to her court, "Yes, I should write a book." I envisioned myself, high and mighty in my queendom, looking upon my subjects from my privileged balcony, knowing that they would clamor for my wisdom. "Oh, Mighty Queen, share your wisdom with us," they'd implore. It was a narcissistic fantasy, and while entertaining to my mind, I'm not driven by flattery and narcissism, so the idea floated around for a while but didn't get much traction.

When the idea of writing a book resurfaced, it was more than a book to me. It was the legacy I would leave my daughters. It was personal. My audience of two might not even care about it today, but one day . . . I hoped they'd pick it up, hear my voice, and feel my presence. One day, my energy would infuse them just as the energy of the Camino pilgrims had filled me during my first night in the Roncesvalles refugio. I realized that, if I gave up on this legacy, I might feel some mild relief in ten minutes, I might accomplish a few extra "mom" tasks in ten months and feel some mild discomfort at not having followed through, but in ten years, I would feel deep regret at having not captured my story and process for my daughters. I also considered how I would let down the number of Supporters who had encouraged me to continue, had routinely asked me how it was coming along, and had requested a first copy because they had an idea they wanted to launch. Then I had a good cry, jumped off my fence, and I wrote this chapter.

Commitment to arrive at the destination is tenuous. It is a choice that is made in each day and moment. Just for today, *commit to going and go!* Don't overthink it. Jump off the fence, step onto your path, and don't look back. Say, "I'm going to Santiago," whatever your Santiago may be. Without commitment to the destination, your chance of success is not just limited, it is nonexistent.

SEVEN
GETTING THERE TOGETHER

Susan and I left the refugio with several other pilgrims, including Christine and Judy, and started walking to Pamplona en route to Santiago. The first couple of days were really fun. Susan and I hadn't seen each other in over a year, and we caught up on each other's lives. After the second day, issues arose for many of the pilgrims. Christine and Judy discovered their packs were too heavy and mailed half of their gear to Santiago to retrieve when they arrived. Susan and I also had challenges. I had trouble matching her stride. Susan is eight inches taller than me—all in her legs. My short legs couldn't keep up. When I tried, my hips hurt, my calf muscles felt like they were on fire, and my lower back ached. Likewise, it was just as difficult for Susan to slow down and take shorter strides.

During a normal day-hike, the difference would not have been an issue. We realized continuing to walk together eight hours per day with twenty pounds on our backs for another thirty days in this same manner would not only be painful but might also lead to injury. We were dismayed because we had looked forward to walking together. Time with Susan had become a part of the Camino experience for me. Also, I was nervous about walking alone. Eventually we made the hard decision to walk separately, each at her own pace. Still, we agreed to arrive in Santiago together.

Susan and I established some guiding principles to help us "walk together" while walking separately. If we hadn't committed to them, it would have been frightfully easy, in a time before abundant cell phone coverage, to become separated, because we could have stopped at different towns or refugios along the way and ended up days apart. Our principles were rooted in clear communication.

First, we determined what was most important: Our long-term goal of getting to Santiago and our daily plan to get there. When we arose in the morning, we reminded each other of the selected destination for the day. Each time we passed each other along the path, we confirmed it. Second, we had a ritual of a morning coffee. At the first town with an open café, Susan would stop to have a coffee and wait for me to arrive. Even though I would leave the refugio and start walking before she did in the morning, Susan would quickly overtake me on the Camino, so she would arrive at the café before me, drink her coffee, and wait for me. By the time I caught up, she was ready to move on, but we'd have a quick moment to check in with how each other was faring, offer each other "¡Buen Camino!"—the pilgrim's greeting on the Camino, which means "Good Journey!"— and Susan would be on her way as I sat down for my break. Third, every night before bed, we scanned our map and planned the next day. We selected the town and refugio to meet in. We promised, no matter how tired we were, even if we thought we couldn't continue on, we would make it to the designated location. We trusted each other to follow through on our commitment. We knew that, if we didn't follow through, we would become separated.

These three guiding principles were how we stayed connected and became our routine for the remainder of the Camino.

LESSON SEVEN
Say What Needs to Be Said

Difficult conversations come in all shapes and sizes. When I realized that Susan and I couldn't walk together, I felt like the wind had been knocked out of me.

It was awkward. I had invited her to walk the Camino with me. While I knew that I didn't know much about hiking in general or walking the Camino in particular, I never expected that Susan and I wouldn't be able to walk together. It had never occurred to me. I may have planned differently if I had known. It was the epitome of the Robert Burns quote, "The best-laid plans of mice and men" often go awry. However, when we create a New Reality, the experience of "This isn't going exactly as I thought it would" is actually quite common as we move toward our destinations; some of the people who accompany us may take different approaches to getting there. At times, we can't distinguish between the what and the how. For me, they have often been the same. "Getting to Santiago" actually meant "Getting to Santiago with Susan," which meant "Getting to Santiago with Susan by walking with Susan every day." I wasn't even conscious of the assumption until it was tested.

Too often, we avoid the awkward situation, the elephant in the room—the obvious, yet unspoken, problem, issue, or challenge. Avoidance is driven by many factors, from a desire to not screw up a relationship to just finishing a project. We have a need to belong that goes beyond it feels good to belong. We are tribal animals for a reason. Isolated humans didn't make it. Conflict and discord threaten belonging and, at a primitive level, survival. We don't like to engage in situations which may challenge belonging. It takes time to engage, time that could be dedicated to completing the task at hand. I often observe executives and teams avoid difficult conversations because they believe it will preserve harmony. I also experience it in my personal relationships. But it isn't useful. Whether large or small, elephants can crush relationships.

For years, I avoided and postponed the difficult conversations in my life until I erupted like Mt. Vesuvius, leaving a wake of destruction. I operated from my fear of the consequences of not looking good and ending up alone. I put on the happy face I learned in my family. We either stuffed our feelings or exploded, and stuffing our feelings was preferred because the explosions were pretty nasty. I was skilled at *looking good*. I'm sure I had Malcolm Gladwell's 10,000 hours of mastery[6] in looking good by the time I was twelve. I hadn't learned any other way and, consequently, was not skilled in working through conflict, large or small. I caused damage both when I erupted and when I stuffed my feelings.

When I erupt, I hurl verbal grenades that cause real damage. They leave emotional bruises and scars. While some truth might exist in what I say, it is a partial truth because my thinking is distorted. *I* feel hurt by the receiver, and *I* act in retaliation. I may have a moment of satisfaction or relief, because I've finally gotten it off my chest and said what it was that most upset me, but I've included a few choice insults in the process. After, I feel terrible regret and embarrassment for what I've said and how I've said it. Further, I feel uncomfortable being around them because of it and may even avoid them. Meanwhile, they are hurt by my words and don't want to be around me (and may also be embarrassed by how they responded to me), leaving us with even more separation and distance—and less connection and belonging—than where we started.

Ironically, when I try a different tack and suppress my feelings and say nothing, I feel terrible regret for being inauthentic, lacking courage to speak my truth, carrying around the burden of my dirty little secret—I'm actually pissed off at myself for not saying I am pissed off at them. It eats at me: I don't like who I am, and I don't like who they are, leaving us, once again, with distance and separation, not connection and belonging.

Neither way is useful. When I erupt, the other person literally knows that I am pissed off, but when I say nothing, they also know something is wrong. Yes, they know then, too. Haven't you had those moments when you can't explain it, but you *just know* your friend is angry with you? She might say all of the right things, but you know she is pissed off. A week goes by, and she finally tells you why. You are stuck between a rock and hard place. Say something unskillfully, and you could damage how you feel about yourself and damage the relationship. Don't say anything at all, and you could still damage how you feel about yourself and damage the relationship.

Whether the dilemma you face is a mild issue or a major concern, tension exists. And this is when the elephant appears. We've already established that burying your thoughts and feelings about the conflict to preserve the relationship won't work. What can you do instead?

A **Productive Dialogue** is required. Productive Dialogue is a conversation between two or more people where conflict exists, the stakes are high, and a positive conclusion is reached. It is the skillful way to work through a difficult topic while building greater trust, commitment, and accountability. It's comprised of four Cs: Context (the desired outcome), Consent (willingness to participate), Content (what needs to be discussed), and Conclusion (the resolution and next steps).

Compare this to a difficult conversation where the subject is awkward or difficult (which is often due to conflicting perceptions, feelings, and values). I joke with my clients that most difficult conversations start with some version of "You have wronged me," which I refer to as the **Content** of the disagreement. You, the perpetrator with your bad behavior, have wronged me, the victim. This is pretty much it. It rarely goes well from there, no matter what the actual word choice for expressing it.

Before launching into Content, Productive Dialogue requires Context and Consent. **Context** is the shared goal or outcome you are both trying to achieve. It is the Vision for your conversation, the positive outcome you want to create. We often forget what we truly want when we launch into Content. **Consent** is the question asked to create psychological safety for the conversation. Prior to my marriage, my friend Doug suggested one simple step to prevent me from exploding at my husband, "Ask him if he'd be willing to have a conversation with you about your concern. Ninety percent of the time, he'll say, 'Let's talk now,'" and Doug was right. What I didn't know then is that decisions are made in the Prefrontal Cortex (PFC) and hippocampus. Decisions are not made in the amygdala which is one of the most primitive parts of the brain. It's the amygdala that takes over and reacts in times of stress or conflict. When I hurl mean-spirited Content at someone from my amygdala, their amygdala reacts. Asking a simple question that requires a decision (like "Would you be willing to talk?") moves both speaker and listener to the PFC, where rational thought is available. With Context and Consent, your listener is two steps closer to having a productive dialogue with you, leading to a positive **Conclusion.**

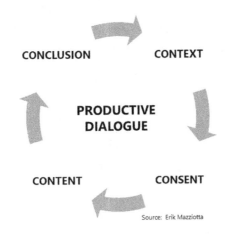

CONCLUSION   CONTEXT

PRODUCTIVE DIALOGUE

CONTENT   CONSENT

Source: Erik Mazziotta

If you were to think of it visually, you would see a loop where, in the upper right, Context leads to affirmative Consent, which enables us to enter into the Content of the difficult conversation, which eventually leads to a more useful Conclusion.[7] Specifically, when entering the Content phase of the conversation, start by ASKING questions, instead of just launching into how you've been wronged. I'm not suggesting that you shouldn't express yourself. Instead, I am saying that timing matters. By seeking the other person's perspective, you learn how she views the situation. You discover if you've missed any relevant information. Maybe you'll realize she hasn't intentionally let you down. With better information, you may be more open to working together to find a good solution. Or you can express how you feel about your shared goal—whether you think you've performed well together. Then she should have a clearer idea of how you see the situation. This may ultimately change her perspective.

Along the Camino, this kind of dialogue might have sounded like:

> Susan: Shannon, I know we both want to get to Santiago together in thirty days. (Context) When would you like to have a conversation about how we are doing? (Consent)

> Me: How about now?

> Susan: Great! How do you think we are doing?" (Content: Seeking perspective)

> Me: Well, I know we are only a couple of days in and, clearly, I don't know that much about the Camino or hiking, but it seems like our pace is probably about right to get there in thirty days. We might even make it in twenty-seven days at this pace.

> Susan: Yes, we might. I noticed you developed two blisters today. The hospitaleros say it is typical to get one or two as you start out. It should clear up soon, but I wondered how you are feeling overall?

> Me: Now that you ask, my hips and shins are killing me. It just seems weird, almost like I'm walking too fast. How about you?

> Susan: It's actually why I'm asking. I'm sore, too, but not just regular muscle aches, it's in my joints. My back doesn't feel right and my hips hurt too. I hate to say it, but I feel like I'm walking too slowly.

Me: Wow, I was thinking I'm walking too fast!

Susan: I hate to tell you this, but I've done a lot of hiking, and I don't know if we can keep walking like this for another twenty-eight days—you walking too fast, me walking too slow. I think we have to figure out another plan. (Conclusion)

Saying what needs to be said is critical. Skillful communication is the key to ensuring success in relationships and results. The four Cs of Productive Dialogue provide a framework to support it. Continued practice surfaces minor differences of opinion before they can become major conflicts. To *WE the Change* and achieve commitment, accountability, or results,[8] you will work with others, so developing skillful communication must be a priority.

EIGHT
VIGILANCE

Susan and I quickly adjusted to our new approach of getting there together by walking separately. I had a daily routine within our shared approach. I woke up each morning at 5 a.m. First priority, take ibuprofen. I did this to prepare my feet, which were covered in blisters and continually throbbed. Then, I would have a light breakfast, check my map, and remind myself where I planned to meet Susan. When I stopped for coffee and to eat a snack, I would check my feet, letting them air a little bit.

I was careful about my feet and continually looked for signs of infection. A simple infection can lead to blood infection, and if a hospitalero discovers it and shares it with a Camino doctor, the Camino is over for you. Pilgrims with seemingly minor health issues are often sent home because of those before them who have died from infection. Therefore, I knew to be vigilant about my feet. In fact, I learned so much about healing feet, I became the healer of others. (Sadly, my foot-healing skills aren't valued in my current profession.)

After my coffee, I walked and walked and walked. In addition to my blisters, the path held other challenges—directions and dogs. I was anxious about directions. I am mildly dyslexic and can transpose numbers and directions when I don't pay careful attention. But on the Camino, my mind easily wandered amidst the monotony of walking *hour after hour, day after day. To get to Santiago, I had to rigorously follow the flechas amarillas (yellow arrows) and Camino scallop shells—markers along the Camino pointing toward Santiago. They confirm you are following the right path. Some markers are obvious, while others are not. I became lost once and had to backtrack an hour to find the right marker. Losing your way on the path also means that you are in less traveled areas. Wild dogs roam the Camino, and pilgrims have been attacked. I knew that staying on the path ensured that if I were attacked and left injured or bleeding or worse, eventually someone would find me. Concerns about blisters, dogs, and directions gnawed at the back of my mind. I learned that if I didn't see an arrow or shell every couple of hours, I had better head back to the last marker I had seen. Without the arrows and shells, I could have wandered, uncertain of my direction.*

When I did finally arrive at our designated refugio each day, I would find the bed that Susan had saved for me when she arrived. (If I hadn't invited Susan, I would have slept on the floor most nights. Inviting others pays off in unexpected ways.) Upon claiming my bed, I would shower, wash my clothes, prepare my feet (AGAIN), get lunch, shop for the night's dinner and the next day's breakfast, rest, eat dinner, and then share my evening with new friends. Around 8 p.m., I would pop in my ear plugs to eliminate the impact of others' snoring and go to sleep, knowing I was one day closer to Santiago.

LESSON EIGHT
Seek the Signals and Signposts

I had moments of trepidation as I ventured out alone on the Camino path. My fears about my own inadequacies were in high gear. It was up to me to find my way on my own and, as I've already established, I knew squat about hiking. *What if I get lost?* (It was a time before cellphones were customary.) "How would I know if I was lost? How would Susan know if I was lost? HOW WOULD ANYONE KNOW IF I WAS LOST?" My mind screamed out of control as it spun an incredible story of how I'd be attacked by a pack of wild dogs, left to die alone in the wilderness of Spain called the Camino.

Awareness of the signs that indicate we are on the right path is critical. Clear thinking is required to see them. While the daily grind may obstruct our immediate view of progress, our mind spinning out of control certainly does. A primary trigger, such as an event or situation that causes a strong emotional reaction internally, is uncertainty. Launching a Big Idea is loaded with it. The fear of the unknown may be the fundamental fear that drives all other fears.[9] The impact? Fear and its irksome sister, anxiety, diminish perception, cognition, creativity, and ability to collaborate.[10] Meanwhile, all those aspects are desirable to create the best results. So, we must not tolerate fear or anxiety. To ward off anxiety, we often employ tried and true strategies of fight, flight, freeze, or flock (aka *"F"ing it up*). Fight shouts, "Get busy. Do something. Do anything." Flight bellows, "Abandon ship!" Freeze whispers, "Stop, wait, hold on," sending a chill up our spine and immobilizing us like an iceberg. Flock compels us to find others who share our anxiety, so that we might wallow in it together.

In the midst of ambiguity, I most often employ Fight to manage my anxiety and fear associated with thoughts or statements such as "I have no idea where to begin. I have no idea what I'm doing. I am lost." When I'm unaware of my anxiety, I react by responding to distractions. I act without paying attention to what is happening in my environment. Quite literally, along the Camino, I missed the yellow arrows when I was busy, lost in my thoughts, not paying attention. It's not only how I responded when walking the Camino but also how I respond in general. When I create a New Reality, such as writing a book, I feel disoriented at the beginning and swirl in *busyness*. The more ambiguous the project, the busier I become. In fact, I've personified this state of being as an entity separate from myself I've named "Busy." Busy is a clever fellow. He starts out as a darling, baby fluffball of a gremlin and develops into a mini-monster, taking me off track. Suddenly, I feel as if I've been slammed against a wall and am out of breath from the many distractions. I have a hard time sitting quietly with the ambiguity and allowing clarity to emerge. Busyness is an odd way to procrastinate on the real work to be done. However, it isn't surprising when I realize I stay busy to continually look good for others. It is a persistent and vicious circle.

If I am highly stressed and not at my best, Fight doesn't always look like Busy. Fight can also mean a sharp tongue, criticism, dismissiveness to others, etc. It isn't how I want to behave. About twenty years ago, I discovered through a self-assessment tool that I often appear remarkably different in high-stress versus low-stress situations. Think Jekyll and Hyde. In normal circumstances, I open conversations with a warm, friendly tone and inquire about you and your life. Under stress, the niceties go out the window, and I begin barking orders. I exhibit no interest in you. This confuses people and most assume it has to do with them, rather than me. "Why is she pissed off at me? What did I do?" Discovering this has enabled me to give a heads-up to others.

With vulnerability, I have shared this true, but not so fun, fact with my colleagues and have given them permission to call me on it. I remember once at Microsoft when my intern, Ursula, had the courage to point it out. I walked into the office completely unaware of my mood and behavior. I was in my third trimester of pregnancy and preparing to launch a leadership program. I had a meeting that morning with the VP of Latin America and his leadership team. I was anxious. I don't remember what I said to Ursula as I passed her in the hallway, but I was gruff and unpleasant. Ursula stepped in front of me and, with kindness and humor, said, "Well hello. I've heard about you. Where did you put her?" Puzzled, I stopped. Ursula continued, "Are you feeling stressed, Shannon? You don't seem like yourself." And it hit me. I understood her and burst out laughing. She added, "So, this is what it looks like when you are stressed. I see what you mean. What can I do right now to help you?" Ursula's ability to *name it to tame it* in the moment when it was most needed changed the course of my day and created a better environment for all around me in the moment.

In the midst of being triggered and "F"ing things up, Ursula created a space for me to **Pause**, **Reflect**, and **Choose**. As I've become more aware of my triggers and responses, I've learned to do this for myself. Consider this example: My boss didn't say hello this morning and my first thought is, "She is ignoring me, she doesn't like my work, and I need to find others who support my ideas." I make up an entire story for why that might be true. Instead, I take a breath and pause. Next, I reflect on my interpretation of the event and ask myself what other interpretations are possible. Finally, I think about other ways to respond and choose the one that enables me to be at my best in the moment.

Fortunately, both my personal self-awareness and my professional experience help me to employ strategies like Pause, Reflect, and Choose to stay on track. These techniques help me to see the signs, because I am calm and centered and able to engage both the right and left hemispheres of my brain. The right side pays attention to intuitive hits or signs, telling me I'm on the right path. The left side builds project plans that track my progress, proving I'm on the right path.

On the right side, the intuitive signs follow one of three patterns: visceral response; rule of threes; and volunteers. Visceral response often starts with physical trembling, even shaking, followed by a sense of disorientation or confusion, and then tearing up or crying. Occasionally, it starts with a voice that seems to leap from my heart, and it shouts, "Yes!" It's as if my body understands the message before my mind knows it. The visceral response is the one that gets my attention the fastest. It throws me off-center and I say, "What the heck just happened to me?" It was present when I met my husband. It prompted me to walk the Camino. It called me to leave the security of a corporate gig.

The rule of threes is more subtle, but I usually notice it. I keep bumping into the same person. First at the grocery store, "Hi, I haven't seen you in a while." Second at the dentist's office, "Wait, we go to the same dentist?" Third at a conference I wouldn't expect her to attend, "Funny meeting you here." I have a rule. Bump into a person three times, schedule a time to get together, even if I don't know the person well. I believe the Universe is telling me to learn from the individual, vice versa, or both. Likewise, when the same idea or challenge presents itself three different times, I view it as a sign to pay attention. I ask myself, "What do I need to know now?" or "What do I need to know about this person now?" I make a point of discovering what I am supposed to learn.

The sign I am most likely to miss is the volunteers. These are people who show genuine interest in my idea and voluntarily ask how they can help. When it does occur to me that someone has volunteered to help me create my New Reality, I am humbled. Volunteers deserve respect for their commitment and dedication to the call of another. Recognizing the volunteers has uplifted me in moments of exhaustion. Their belief in the idea energizes me. I also become more conscious of how my behavior impacts them. I do what I can to uplift them as well.

Some signals arise spontaneously, while others can be planned. Being aware of both kinds accelerates our progress. Pause, Reflect, and Choose also enable me to slow down, engage my left brain and keep my plans moving forward. The left brain develops step-by-step project plans, which I learned to do as a professional consultant. My husband jokes, "You can create an Excel spreadsheet for anything." Christmas dinner for twenty—check! Here's the plan. Packing for vacation—check! Here's the plan. Making school lunches—check! Here's the plan.

I learned early in my consulting career, promotions come to those who deliver on time and under budget. Good planning helped me get promoted. Having a plan with agreed-upon milestones is critical when the daily grind gets in the way of being able to see immediate progress. Here's why. Without a path, without a plan, without milestones, it's *just* one more good idea, and it's easy to get lost. As you begin to launch your Big Idea or create your New Reality, you start in a place of innocence and ambiguity. Even if you have some experience, you haven't quite done "this" before. If you had, you would most likely be finished and wouldn't be exploring how to create *your* New Reality. Knowing your destination and knowing how to get there are two vastly different pursuits.

I am a stickler for plans and milestones and hate missing deliverable dates. It's like a house of cards. Knock one out of place and the house collapses. Miss one milestone, and it becomes easier to miss the next one and the one after. In most change projects, the big milestones are aligned with the ending of one of the primary phases of Analyze the Current State, Create the Vision, Build the Implementation Plan, Begin Implementation. Each one of those phases includes smaller steps that must be performed to complete the particular phase.

When moving toward your destination, setting small goals that you can quickly accomplish gives you a sense of momentum. I tell my clients, "Baby steps become journeys." Ask yourself, "What am I going to do today to move myself in the right direction?" Some people use mind-mapping as a way to brainstorm their ideas. I like flip chart paper and sticky notes. I write one step/idea per sticky note about how to get started and randomly attach these ideas to the flip chart paper. It starts out pretty messy. But once I have my notes on the paper, I group and sequence them into phases. I'll even ask others to take a look at it and share their ideas to help me figure out what I might be missing. Eventually, it organizes itself into a project plan. Before starting the Camino, I brainstormed a set of activities similar to the picture below and then organized them into phases: learn about the Camino; check in with Susan; and Madrid to Roncesvalles.

Project X: How to Start the Camino

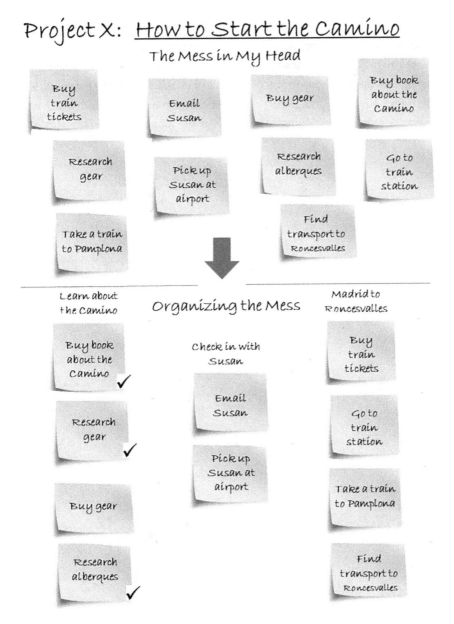

When I finish, I tell people about my plan and milestones, because it keeps me honest and on track. I feel accountable to others, not just myself, because people ask, "How's the idea coming along?" It helps to maintain focus, motivation, and momentum when I complete each milestone activity.

Look for the signs or markers indicating that you are moving in the right direction. If you are honest with yourself, you may see them but choose to ignore them. Down deep, most of us know when it is time to move to our next destination, but we choose not to. We can just as easily choose to pay attention and follow the signs. Integrating the right- and left-brain approaches is when you can accelerate your ability to launch your Big Idea or create a New Reality.

NINE
NO PAIN, NO GAIN

By the tenth day of the Camino, I had mastered my daily routine and I was entering Burgos, the place I would reunite with Joe. Shortly after I made the decision to go to Santiago, I called him to share my decision to continue to Santiago. He was tremendously supportive and planned to meet me for an evening in Burgos. He drove to Burgos from Madrid in about two hours. In the world of the Camino, I found this somewhat surreal. I would walk eight hours to travel fifteen miles. Joe would drive two hours to travel 150. It had taken me the equivalent of ten days to travel from Madrid to Burgos via the Camino. While Susan and our new friend, Lori, sought out the local refugio, Joe and I found a cozy hotel. I was delighted to see him, and I was overjoyed at the prospect of a warm, soothing bath.

As I prepared to soak, I called Joe into the bathroom to observe my twice-daily ritual of caring for my feet. Seeking sympathy, I showed him the damage. Once beautifully pedicured tiny feet had transformed into oozing, broken down, primitive stumps. I told him about the trials of the Camino and how I walked in spite of the pain, the rain, and the lightning storms that we had experienced that morning. I explained what it meant to be a pilgrim and how I had done this every day. **Every day.** I waited for him to agree that I was indeed brave for carrying on in spite of it all.

My marine looked at me and said, "What were you thinking? It wouldn't be a pilgrimage if it weren't challenging." A bolt of anger flew up my spine. I'm sure he read it all over my face as he nonchalantly exited the bathroom. **What did he just say?** *This was not the response I was looking for. I couldn't believe how he casually tossed out his feedback. I fumed, "Typical male, absolutely no empathy. He doesn't understand what this is all about." I was so angry! I managed to settle myself down so we could enjoy the evening together, but his comment burned inside me.*

The next day, immediately after he left, I told Susan and Lori about his insensitivity. I said in a sing-songy voice, "It wouldn't be a pilgrimage if it weren't challenging." They were as outraged as I was. **Clearly, he did not understand.** *We talked about his comment, not for several kilometers but rather for* **several days.** *But the more we talked about it, the more it became a mantra when the Camino wasn't going quite as easily as we hoped—"Well, you know, it wouldn't be a pilgrimage if it weren't challenging." When we met pilgrims who had their own stories of woe, we would nod and say, "Well, it wouldn't be a pilgrimage if it weren't challenging!"*

In truth, my husband, the marine, understood better than any of us. **It wouldn't be a pilgrimage if it weren't challenging.** *What none of us knew then: I had yet to see the worst of the Camino.*

LESSON NINE
It Wouldn't Be a Pilgrimage If It Weren't Challenging (aka This Is Hard)

At that time, I resentfully accepted that pain was a part of the process. It would present itself on many fronts—physical, emotional, intellectual, and spiritual. After all, *no pain, no gain.* I didn't realize that, based on the evidence, if I persisted the pain would be temporary, and I would ultimately reach my destination. Instead, I struggled blindly along the Camino, not knowing that my pain was both inevitable and temporary. I wallowed in it, bemoaned my state of affairs and found my flock to commiserate with and keep me on the path. We complained to each other, but we kept going. In our grumbling, we explored what it meant to be a pilgrim on a pilgrimage, and through our conversation, discovered and accepted Joe's wisdom: "It wouldn't be a pilgrimage if it weren't challenging."

If you think getting to the destination is going to be easy, think again. Creation and change are seldom easy. We can pick the destination and follow the markers, but countless examples from legend, myth, and story tell us the hero's journey is fraught with challenges. In fact, without some type of adversity to overcome, I question whether real change is even possible. Evidence supports this. Across cultures, we observe a documented pattern of how individuals and even organizations, when called to create new realities, experience and struggle with challenges. Eventually, they overcome them to succeed, gaining new levels of insight and capability in the process.

In the 1800s, the German anthropologist Adolph Bastian noticed that myths from all over the world were built from the same elementary ideas. Later, Swiss psychiatrist Carl Jung named them archetypes, which he believed to be the building blocks not only of the unconscious mind, but of a collective unconscious. Jung believed that we are all born with the same basic subconscious model of what makes a hero, mentor, or quest, and that's why people who don't speak the same language can enjoy the same stories. Finally, Joseph Campbell, in his book *The Hero with a Thousand Faces,* mapped the archetypes to stories from religion and myths around the world, found the common pattern he called the monomyth, and named it the *Hero's Journey.*[11] He documented at least one story of a hero on a quest in every culture and religion. Some shared characteristics that he found across cultures are:

- The hero's story always includes an important rite of passage.
- Each hero's journey is personal and unique to his/her particular challenges and circumstances.
- Each hero recognizes and learns to use one or more unique gifts.
- The successful execution of this gift is critical to the population's welfare, perhaps even survival.[12]

After completing the Camino and discovering Campbell's work, I was inspired to create a leadership development workshop for Microsoft to help leaders improve their effectiveness during times of change. *Accelerating Transitions* was the practical result—a two-day workshop integrating my learning from the Camino with Campbell's work. While developing the workshop, I heard of Lorna Catford and Michael Ray's class on creativity and innovation, taught at Stanford University business school, based on the Hero's Journey. They observed, "The hero often does not seem particularly heroic at first. In the course of meeting a challenge that disrupts an initial state of innocence, the hero is initiated into a realm where grave danger lurks. With the assistance of allies, the hero breaks out of that world to successfully meet the challenge and return home with a gift of treasure or wisdom. The hero's return is celebrated, and life is resumed—somehow transformed by the hero's journey."[13]

In their work, they depicted the Hero's Journey in a U-shape pattern with six distinct steps, or phases:[14]

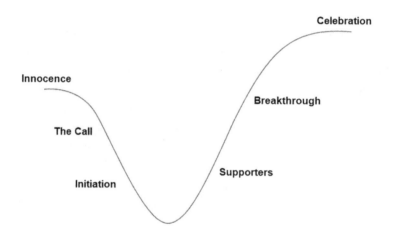

- **Innocence**—a starting point, an inner state of being or naivete.
- **The Call** (to adventure)—a crisis or a desire to see or do something special that taps a deeper motivation or yearning that "calls" our hero to leave her comfortable world. Sometimes, as in my case, it seems there is no choice but to answer it . . . to stay where the hero is becomes less and less an option or just increasingly uncomfortable.

- **Initiation**—more than just a step, initiation is almost a process or journey unto itself. It is about discovering what you don't know and learning an entirely new way of operating. It often includes several smaller adventures and challenges but also moments for fun and rest. The tension is mounting and the challenges get harder with no guarantee that everything will work out in the end. This step brings an intriguing paradox: while ultimate success or failure hangs on the hero's shoulders, a point of surrender is required to begin the climb up the curve.
- **Supporters**—referred to as Allies by Catford and Ray. Contrary to popular wisdom, no hero succeeds alone. Supporters and companions accompany her on the journey and often appear at critical moments when all seems lost. They sustain and recharge a worn-out hero to enable her to finish the impossible task she has set out to do.
- **Breakthrough**—the situation takes a turn for the better. The hero's task is completed successfully. The hero is transformed by this quest into a new woman who has full realization of her unique skills and becomes masterful in applying them in the service of others.
- **Celebration**—the hero returns home. She is recognized as someone of status and importance and is often called upon to continue applying her gifts to the tribe or community in which she lives . . . though not necessarily in such a dramatic way as before.

Knowing the path of the hero has helped me tremendously over time. Being familiar with each of the stages has strengthened my approach to managing change projects. By identifying my place on the path, I am more able to leverage the gifts and address the challenges each stage presents, leading to greater likelihood of completing the project. Looking back at the part of the Camino where I entered Burgos to meet Joe, if I were to plot myself along the Hero's Journey U-curve, I would say I was firmly situated in Initiation: I was learning the Camino, my own strengths and liabilities as I maneuvered the path, and how to be present to the lessons it offered. I wonder where you would place yourself at this time on your own Hero's Journey? How could this knowledge support you in launching your Big Idea or creating your New Reality?

TEN
SURRENDER

The path beyond Burgos would become the most difficult stretch of the Camino for me. The distance between Burgos and Leon was flat, hot, and covered as far as the eye could see with wheat fields. It would take ten days to walk the distance before we reached the foothills of Galicia. Being from South Dakota, I know wheat fields. By this time, I had at least twelve of the sixteen blisters I would eventually experience. I was now in relentless pain, and I walked alone. Being of fairly average height, Susan usually walked with others. I, on the other hand, had no company, because my stride was shorter and my pace was slower than average. The wheat fields drew me right into my childhood, which was less than ideal. I spent most of my childhood ashamed of my family situation and trying to hide it from my friends.

Externally, my homelife most likely appeared creative and intellectual. My parents painted our family home tangerine orange, with flag blue trim. It was known as the "Home of the Great Pumpkin" and had a graffiti room inside where the dining room was meant to be. Individuals could share their thought-provoking sentiments on our walls. Each statement had to be approved by my parents since they didn't allow profanity of any type. They were proud that Russell Means, an Oglala Lakota activist, had signed our wall. My siblings and I were known as overachievers in our community. We "looked good," which contributed to the external appearance. Internally, and for the better part of my childhood, my family was impacted by mental illness, alcoholism, abandonment, and financial insecurity. As the family dynamic spiraled downward and the family structure fractured, we became more internally focused and had little besides each other. I was the oldest child, who filled in the parental gaps. As I walked through the wheat fields between Burgos and Leon, I was stuck in the mire, thinking of my childhood with no escape.

Then the Day of Devils arrived, a distance of more than twenty kilometers during which pilgrims walk with little access to shade and no access to well water. This was a particularly bad day for me.

On the Day of Devils, I was contemplating the three "truths" pilgrims hear when traveling the Camino. First, the Camino calls you. I absolutely believe that one. Second, everyone's Camino is different. I was living it. From my perspective, Susan was having a jolly time with her walking companions. Third, the Camino is a metaphor for life. If true—my life was about pain and being alone. I didn't like the implications. I was at my lowest point emotionally. The physical agony of the blisters under the searing sun and obvious isolation from my friends tormented me.

The emotional hell I put myself through as I considered these three "truths" of the Camino dwarfed the physical experience. I wallowed in the anguish of my past—from my childhood to my recent miscarriages to my mother's cancer. As I dug deep into my history, I looked in front of me and saw nothing and nobody. I looked behind me and saw nothing and nobody, except wheat fields, for what seemed like miles. It confirmed my belief that I was alone in the world, abandoned by all.

I felt so hurt and angry. I was particularly mad at God for allowing this torture in my life. I felt sorry for myself. Like a three-year-old experiencing a tantrum, I literally threw my arms to the sky and shook my walking stick wildly at the heavens and screamed. I pounded it on the ground multiple times with all of my force and cried, "If the Camino is a metaphor for life, why is my life so filled with pain?" I cried, screamed, and doubled over in despair, thinking that if I gave up, no one would even find me until the next day, because I was usually the last one to arrive.

In my misery, I seriously contemplated dissolving into the wheat fields and waiting for wild dogs to materialize and attack. In the frenzy I created in my mind, I believed no one would even notice or care that I was missing. Finally, in exhaustion after fighting metaphorical windmills and screaming at the wind, I gave up. I surrendered and said, "I just can't do this, God, because if this is the way it's going to be, if I am going to be alone through all of this pain, well, I just don't want to think about it anymore. I can't do it. I don't know how." I was at the threshold, looking into the abyss, surrendering to my fate, wondering what it might be. Would I plunge into nothingness? Would anyone notice? Would anyone care?

At this moment of surrender, I heard, "¡Buen Camino!" I froze. I thought I was hallucinating because I had just looked behind me and had not seen anyone for miles. Jolted out of my apoplectic frenzy, I took two tentative steps forward. Again, I heard, "¡Buen Camino!"—but closer. I still had tears, mixed with the dust of the arid land, running down my face, and I was shaking as I thought, "No, I am definitely hallucinating because of the heat." But as I thought this, I slowly turned around and several yards behind me I saw an older woman approaching. I had seen her a few times in prior days. She was in her sixties and she kept to herself. She was moving quickly.

My mind was racing, "Where did she come from? Did she see my wild display? She had to have seen me. This is so humiliating." As she approached me, she again offered, "¡Buen Camino!" I was so embarrassed and could barely make eye contact. I motioned for her to pass me because the whole world seemed to pass me on the Camino. Nobody walked at my pace. But she slowed down to walk with me. Irritated and self-conscious I thought, "Of all days, someone wants to walk with me."

Once more, she softly said, "¡Buen Camino!"

I thought, disgustedly, "Yeah! ¡Buen Camino! all right." Instead I said to her, "You know, I am ready to die."

She looked at me and said, "It's not your day to die."

I looked at her quizzically. "What?" I croaked. The word barely passed my lips.

She pointed to a marker on the road that I had not yet noticed and seemed to appear from nowhere. Markers are placed on the Camino where pilgrims have died. They are not common, but they are occasional reminders that not all make it. She pointed to the marker and said, "It was his day to die. It is not your day to die, for I am here to walk with you."

I started to tremble and cry. A new truth had been revealed. The lies I had told myself in the spiral of defeat—I was not good enough, I was not worthy, I was alone—were obliterated in that moment. God revealed Himself to me in the stranger on the road and said, "I've been right here, by your side. You have never been alone."

How could I be so sure? She materialized out of thin air! At my lowest moment. When, in my arrogance, I was certain of my separation from all belongingness, compassion, and love, God had been with me—I had never been alone.

We walked together. This beautiful soul, whom I had shamefully avoided at the refugios because she had appeared strange in her solitude and quiet observation of the pilgrims, walked with me. She had an incredible, dark sense of humor. She told me stories and made me laugh for the next two hours.

At one point I asked her, "Why are you walking with me? No one walks with me."

"Every day, I get up and I look for the person who needs me," she replied, "and I knew today was your day—that you would need me."

I was stunned. Her words gutted me. I wanted to sink to the ground in the depth of my embarrassment for ever having doubted God's love for me. "It is not your day to die, for I am here to walk with you."

She was an amazing woman—one who knew her role and how to serve and was guided to me. And on that day, she couldn't have been more right in the course of her ministry. In those few hours I spent with her, the only detail I learned about her was that she was from Germany. I don't even remember her name. She stayed with me for only one day. After that, I don't know what happened to her. I do *believe God worked through her, because from that day forward, I have never felt alone.*

LESSON TEN
Face Your Dragons

The moment the German pilgrim showed up has been, to date, one of the most profound experiences in my life. I reflect on it most days and marvel at what happened to me. I've asked myself more than once, "Did I hallucinate? Did it happen?" But that incident is as true to me as the love I have for my daughters. I experienced the most profound sense of being loved by something bigger and beyond myself. Plus, Susan and Lori saw her later too; so, I know she was quite real. The experience of being loved and connected to something bigger than myself bonded me to humanity and all living things. My life took on a new meaning, a new purpose, and a new sense of responsibility.

Prior to that experience, I had always had a deep faith in God as I understood God: a greater force of love operating in the world, binding all souls together. I had also witnessed debilitating addiction and mental illness and the impact it could have in my own family, but I was not personally afflicted with either. As the oldest child, I often protected my younger siblings from my parents' arguments and abusive behavior. When their Irish tempers ignited and they hurled every imaginable insult at each other, the force of their combined unbridled energy seemed to rock our foundation. At eight-years-old, I would stand sentry on the staircase landing, peeking over the bannister into our living room and tell my siblings, "It's okay. It's not as bad as it sounds. Go back to bed. It *will* be okay," as their small arms hugged each other close in worry and fear at the top of the stairs. I was the guardian of the innocent, the protector. Even after my father became sober and changed his life and my parents divorced, I continued to play that codependent role by people-pleasing or ignoring my own needs in service of others'. My mother's depression created other issues. In reality, I didn't feel protected or safe. I felt alone in my own home, but I put on a good show for the world outside, for others, so they would think *everything was okay*. I developed a belief that God had gifted me with what I personally needed to be alright. God would be there for others who hadn't received as many gifts or as much emotional strength. He had given me intellectual and emotional fortitude to weather the bad times. I was to rely on myself.

In the moment of profound loneliness on the Camino, I was angry with God, because I recognized that I was no longer capable of *going it alone*. The prior year and a half had pushed me to the edge of a metaphorical cliff, and I was standing precariously at the precipice. My strength alone was not sufficient to address the pain of my past. I felt abandoned at the deepest level. I was done with being alone, but I didn't know how to escape it and viewed it as my long-term fate, that is, until the German pilgrim arrived. Her mystical appearance at the exact moment of my surrender, at the lowest point of my despair, meant *I had never been alone*. It was the only explanation that made sense to me. The ultimate Protector had never abandoned me. Still, I had immediately tried to push my would-be companion away, motioning for her to pass me on the path. When she refused, I reluctantly accepted her support. As we walked together and she shared her wisdom and humor, I came to not only value her support but also realize that I needed it. It was time for me to let down my guard. The awareness that I was not alone and its accompanying mindset shift changed how I viewed *everything* that had happened before and how I would view *everything* moving forward.

All journeys to the destination will have moments of despair. I suspect that the level of despair varies by how difficult the journey is. In those moments when we think we cannot go one step further, and we are truly ready to give up, we must have faith that support will materialize. Since then, I have seen similar assistance show up for many people and organizations. Connecting this to the Hero's Journey, I had entered the Pit of Despair, a place between Initiation and Supporters where the hero swings violently between the two. I am reminded of my favorite movie, *The Princess Bride*, and the moment when Westley, the hero, awakes to discover that he is strapped to a table and is in grave danger. He asks the Albino, "Where am I?" to which The Albino, Prince Humperdinck's henchman, responds in a hoarse, gravelly voice, "The Pit of Dehspaihhhhhhhhh."[15] It is not a step like the others but rather an iterative loop, a paradoxical place—the hero has never felt more alone or like her fate (and the fate of the world) is in her own hands.

Before the hero can reach Breakthrough, she must first slide down the U-curve of the Hero's Journey. The force of her descent pushes her momentarily up, toward Supporters, only to fall back to Initiation. As she swings between them, surrender, not force, breaks the cycle. At the point of surrender, transformation occurs. Although not initially obvious, the surrender in the Pit of Despair provides an advantage. On the surface, it may seem like an unnecessary detour or even a step backward, but the situation releases an energy, enabling her to climb the hill of hope to the other side of the U-curve. Supporters arrive. Fate or grace intervenes. On the *Day of Devils*, after entering the Pit of Despair, I had surrendered, and in the most difficult moment, met my Supporter, just as every hero must, in order to achieve breakthrough and celebration. In the Pit, I faced and fought my dragons as the rite of passage to the next stage of my journey.

In the midst of launching your Big Idea or creating your New Reality, and no matter how accomplished you are, you will meet your dragons—challenges, difficulties, or issues where the strengths that made you successful in the past no longer serve you. In *The Power of Myth*, Joseph Campbell viewed the dragon as a symbol of divinity or transcendence. It represents the unity of heaven and earth by combining the serpent form (earthbound) with the bat/bird form (airborne).[16] The dragon is present when you continue to apply what worked in the past but the situation gets worse, not better. Repeating old ways hoping to achieve new results doesn't help you transform and only works to ensure your defeat.

In myth, dragons are found guarding treasure. The bigger the dragon, the bigger the treasure. The hero's journey is based on the premise that each of us arrives in the world with a unique set of gifts as well as limitations. Each hero must discover her special attributes and talents. But she is also obliged to acknowledge how their overuse limits the potential for building new strengths and achieving her true potential. In becoming overly self-reliant, I had changed my situation in life, but I also never learned to acknowledge when I needed help, let alone ask for it. That limited my ability to expand or scale my work, because I didn't know how or when to include others. While self-reliance contributed to my past success, overuse would limit my future success. As I learned to include others, I expanded my sphere of influence, discovered more creative solutions, achieved greater buy-in, and experienced even greater success. I effectively learned to *WE the Change:* work collaboratively with others to deliver the Big Idea and New Reality. Of all the lessons of the Camino, *this is the most important for me.* Today when I am conscious of being stuck, I ask for help. When I forget and find myself relying on old behaviors—and this can still happen when I'm under stress and not conscious—I've learned help will show up anyway and my job is to accept it. Support always comes at the moment it is least expected and from the most unlikely places. The hero's job is to welcome it with gratitude.

Both meeting your dragons and the way you respond to them can determine whether you climb out of the Pit or stall and fail to reach your destination. It is a critical moment, and many projects stop right there, because most people don't know that they must fight the dragons in order to climb the hill of hope. If you didn't know that it is a requirement on the path to your destination, why would you put yourself through this torture? Facing and fighting the dragons head-on is required to complete the journey.

ELEVEN
GRATITUDE

From that moment forward, my Camino experience changed. I accepted it as it was meant to be. I decided that although my Camino was different from others', it was no longer going to be one focused on pain.

The next morning, I still ached. Other pilgrims asked how my feet were doing because I was a novelty. Instead of sharing the details of how many blisters I had and how I cared for them, I answered they were fine and let's talk about something else. I decided that I didn't have to share my misery with everyone. I chose to enjoy what was going on around me, and I walked on to the next town.

In the next refugio, the hospitalera, Laura, looked at my feet while I was cleaning them in the courtyard and asked, "What's wrong with your feet?"

"Nothing's wrong with my feet," I replied. I was on my new path.

She eyed me strangely and said, "No, something is wrong with your feet." I thanked her and explained I was fine.

She stared firmly and said, "No. Something's wrong with your feet. I've walked the Camino three times. Something's definitely wrong with your feet. Come with me."

I felt conflicted and hesitated. I had found courage and peace in accepting my situation and was committed to the positive perspective. It was strange to have finally come to terms with and accept my physical misery and then suddenly realize a respite might be near after all. Laura did not budge. She told me to pick up my boots and follow her. I accepted her help. I was learning.

She escorted me to the town's cobbler, who inspected my boots and declared that the insoles were the wrong size. He showed how the heel of my foot was coming down on the insole incorrectly. He immediately created new ones for me. I had to admit that they felt better.

Next, Laura took me to the pharmacist, who examined my feet and explained I was allergic to the tape holding the gauze patches in place. The red, bumpy, scaly, itchy patches around the blisters were a rash generated by the allergy. She gave me a special cream and hypoallergenic surgical tape. Finally, Laura escorted me to her office at the refugio, where she handed me two of the largest sanitary napkins I had ever seen. I politely declined, explaining I did not need them.

Emphatically she pushed, "No, they're for your sandals. Part of your problem is that your feet aren't getting enough air. Remove the adhesive on the bottom of the pad, put them on the interior base of the sandal, and step into the sandal with the cotton facing up. Try it."

I did as I was told, and it was—heaven. Heaven! I felt like I was walking on marshmallows. Prior to Laura's intervention, I would prepare my feet and then put on my sandals when I arrived at the refugio. My friends would laugh because I would walk hunched over like an old lady because my feet were so tender that I could barely tolerate the pressure to fully stand up. With this innovation, I was prancing down the street, so happy in my sandals cushioned with sanitary napkins.

After meeting Laura, I wasn't suffering as much. Laura helped me to look for ideas outside my comfort zone. I felt pretty silly the first time I put those sanitary napkins in my sandals, but I felt so good that I didn't care what anybody else thought. "Oh, there's that strange American with the blisters and the sanitary napkin sandals."

I wasn't the only one experiencing new approaches to the Camino. My fellow pilgrims and I were suddenly ambushed by high school students who began popping up along the path. Not a few, but many.

To receive a certificate for completing the Camino, a pilgrim must walk a minimum distance of one hundred kilometers, or sixty-two miles, of the path. In the summer, high schools would drop busloads of teenagers along the Camino to walk the minimum, pick up their certificate, and have a noteworthy accomplishment to put on their resumes as they prepared for college applications. For them, the Camino was one big fiesta.

Susan and I had walked over four hundred miles of a tranquil and reflective Camino when the students arrived. Worse, they executed our refugio trick with steroids. Having boundless energy, the niños (children, as we called them) would send a sprinter ahead to grab all the beds. When the "real" pilgrims—Susan, Lori, and those who had started in Roncesvalles—would arrive, the beds would already be gone, and we would either sleep on the floor or walk on to the next town, hoping the other niños had not captured those beds too. It was frustrating, but we kept our humor by adding lines to Susan's new poem, ¿Niños, niños, porqué hay niños?"—"Children, children, why are they here?" We wished that they would go away.

They didn't go away. Instead we learned to adapt. We learned to ask the niños where they thought they might stay at the end of the day and then walk to a different location. We spoke to the hospitaleros who, having walked the Camino, understood our plight and would try to find us the quietest space in the refugio, occasionally offering us their private rooms. In the midst of chaos, we found a new path to tranquility, which guided us during the last miles to our destination.

A week after encountering the teenagers, we arrived in Santiago, and we went immediately to the cathedral. For most pilgrims, this is where their Camino ends. My Camino was not yet finished. When I entered the cathedral, something within me broke, and I started to cry. I actually fell down on my knees in the cathedral. I was so grateful to have made it, but I also knew the experience was not yet complete for me. I had told my friends along the Camino that it was my "3G Camino," meaning "Three Generations": I had walked the Camino for my mother, myself, and my future family.

I did not share how I carried the ultrasounds of the two children that I had miscarried because I did not know how to throw them *away. For months, they had sat on my desk at home, because I didn't know what to do with them. At the cathedral, I wrote a letter to St. James. I put their pictures with the letter, and I turned their souls over to the care of St. James. I explained that I couldn't carry them with me anymore. If I wanted to truly arrive at the destination, I had to let go of them. I placed the letter and their pictures in a box at the cathedral. Instantaneously, I had the most incredible feeling of hope. Interestingly, I hadn't been aware that I had ever lost it. I knew I had been profoundly sad, but I didn't know that hope had vanished. In the moment of letting go, hope returned to me. I knew that I would return to Madrid, and that I would have a family. I had arrived in "Santiago"—both the one on the outside and the one on the inside. I had arrived at **my** destination.*

Although each of our "Santiagos" in life are different, getting to the destination is possible for all of us, if we heed the Camino's lessons. I did get to Santiago. Today, I have a mother who has been free of cancer for nineteen years. I have a wonderful husband who has supported me in each journey I have taken since then. And, I have two beautiful daughters, Savannah and Fiona, who were the inspiration for writing this book. Ultimately . . .

LESSON ELEVEN
Count Your Blessings—Not Your Blisters!

As I entered the last phase of the Camino, my mindset shifted to a focus on the positive instead of the negative. With the shift came a sense of gratitude. Gratitude positively impacts our perception, cognition, creativity, and ability to collaborate, just as threat inversely affects them, as indicated in Chapter Eight.[17] As a result, I became more open to new and creative ideas. However, old habits die hard, and I didn't immediately jump at Laura's offer of help. In fact, my initial reaction was to reject her assistance, to go it alone as I had done before: it would take a lot of practice to say yes to help and, more importantly, to learn to ask for it. Without Laura's encouragement, I would never have discovered the innovations required to ultimately make my journey successful. Laura reminded me of the importance of talking with people we don't normally talk with and trying approaches that seem out of the ordinary, like sanitary napkins as the insoles of our sandals. Learning to allow others to creatively contribute to the "how" of reaching the destination is an important part of the process.

Few successes, if any, happen solely through individual effort. World-class athletes who participate in individual sports such as long-distance running, gymnastics, or downhill skiing are supported by the expertise of coaches, nutritionists, psychologists, and doctors. Their supporters speed up results by bringing best-in-class ideas and innovations to deliver success. I was comfortable practicing this in my work environment on organizational change projects. My clients depended on my ability to seek best practices from other companies and subject matter experts. However, tapping into those resources for my own projects, like walking the Camino, didn't even enter my mind. Sure, I researched what to bring before I left, but once I entered the Camino experience, I became completely unconscious of the benefits of including others. I became so intently mesmerized by my own "stuff" that my perception became quite narrow. Laura's insistence and unique perspective about my situation, combined with a desire to help me succeed, was an important reminder of the power of *WE the Change*. So, connect with people, ask more questions, read new books, listen to a podcast. You never know where the next idea or connection will come from that will move you one step closer to your destination.

Occasionally, even after reaching out to others, I can still feel the need for new approaches to launching my Big Idea. When that happens, I look to the book of my friend Kaihan Krippendorff, *Outthink the Competition,* and the "36 Stratagems"[18] (or stories, found in an ancient Chinese text, the *Thirty-Six Stratagems*). Similar stories that inform strategy, like the Trojan horse, are found in other cultures. The beauty in the 36 Strategems is their completeness. The stories are derived from one-thousand years of military strategies which Krippendorff has adapted to business strategies. They are a complete catalogue of approaches to close the gap between D and V. For example, when we hear Trojan horse, we don't just see a horse; we recall the story of how the Greeks created a giant horse with soldiers hidden inside. The Trojans, viewing it as a victory trophy, pulled it into their city after the Greeks sailed away. Later that night, the hidden Greek soldiers climbed out of it and opened the gates to the city, allowing the Greek army to enter and end the ten-year war. To close the gap, we ask ourselves, "What is our Trojan horse?" How could we adopt and adapt the

Trojan horse idea to get to our destination? It's much faster to adopt and adapt one of the thirty-six stratagems/stories than to attempt to come up with a completely new approach. In fact, research proves that this group of thirty-six are MECE, mutually exclusive—each is different—and collectively exhaustive— no others exist. This is the complete list of options to close the gap. Why not make it easier and begin with them?[19] You can find them at: https://outthinker. com/category/36-stratagems/.

The teenagers who showed up near the end of the Camino were innovative. They also felt like a nuisance. If I had a nickel for every time new Supporters showed up near the end of my projects, I'd be wealthy. Often, the same people who were early Opposers later consider themselves early adopters—people who come on board at the beginning. Initially, I felt resentment toward these young people. They hadn't done the hard work of the Camino. They didn't really know what it took to be a *true* pilgrim and complete the Camino. How foolish I was. Who was I to judge what a true pilgrim or pilgrimage was? They had a different journey from mine, but it was their journey. All journeys involve nuisances along the road. By accepting them, whatever they may be, we can all get to the destination, regardless of our differing intentions. The road needs to be wide enough for all people to reach the destination, and wider still so that we can give way to those who might upset us along the way. After all, the Camino is different for each of us.

The additional supporters near the end of the journey are a declaration of confidence. According to Derek Sivers in his TedTalk and YouTube sensation, *Dancing Guy*, "As more people jump in, it's no longer risky. If they were on the fence before, there's no reason not to join now. They won't be ridiculed, they won't stand out, and they will be part of the in-crowd, if they hurry."[20] These late adopters are foretelling your success, acknowledging that you have been on the right path all along. They come on board because success is near, and they want to be a part of it. You're nearing the finish line. This IS going to happen.

The final stretch of creating a New Reality requires many resources. Many moving parts come together at the same time to *go live*, as we describe it in consulting. As often said, "The devil is in the details." It is much like a wedding day, when each moment is timed perfectly in parallel and in sequence to optimize the event, such as the florist delivering the flowers so they will be perfectly perky during the grand event, the caterers delivering the meal (hot!), the bride arriving at the church without a wrinkle in her dress. At this point in your journey, you have expended a lot of energy doing the heavy lifting. You could use supporters to draft behind, to give yourself a chance to recharge for the last sprint to the finish line. Plus, no doubt, they will make it better by bringing even more new ideas to ensure success.

Without your posse of supporters, you could make it ninety percent of the way, only to completely lose steam and miss the final requirement to dot all of the i's and cross all of the t's. Wallowing in resentment won't serve you. Suggesting through your tone, attitude, or language, "So, now you want to help me? Where were you before, when all of the hard work was going on?" only breeds discord. Trust me, I've made the mistake and learned the hard way. Discord impedes success, or worse, derails it. For the last stretch, you need all hands on deck who are willing to champion and implement your Big Idea or New Reality. Let go of your doubts, so that together, you can *WE the Change*. Embrace these later-coming "early adopters" and give them jobs to better ensure that you deliver success.

Celebrate with them when you arrive at your destination. If you are like me, arriving at the destination can occasionally feel anticlimactic. The build up in your mind doesn't always match the actual experience. You may already be thinking of the NEXT Big Idea. Remember, your Supporters aren't you. In many cases, they have also worked hard and need to know you value their contribution. To make recognition meaningful, consider expectations and needs. To start, make sure people know what is expected of them. Clearly defined and communicated expectations drive excellent performance. Performance without feedback leaves people wondering how they are doing and can negatively impact future performance. Reward individuals who meet or exceed the standards. The standards you set communicate your expectations of others, and these, in turn, affect others' level of aspiration.[21]

Finally, ask what your team members—and especially your Supporters—prefer in the way of recognition. Once, I offered what I thought a team member would appreciate: a large basket of goodies . . . in front of two hundred people. A true introvert, the public display of gratitude was too much for her and actually had the opposite effect. It taught me to research what meaningful recognition looked like for each person on my team. The next time I recognized her, I did it quietly with a thank-you card and a gift card for a lovely dinner for her and her husband at their favorite restaurant.

Don't underestimate the importance of celebration. To engage their continued support, be sure to express gratitude, acknowledging the roles and celebrate the many contributions of your Supporters. And one more thing: Do the same for yourself. **You've made it to your Santiago!**

CONCLUSION
¡BUEN CAMINO!

"**¡B**uen Camino! Do you need some help?" he called from across the path.

"¡Buen Camino! No, I'm good, thanks, just adjusting my boot." In fact, it was a ruse to convince my friends that I needed to stop to check my feet. I told them they could go on without me, and I would catch up a bit later. Actually, I wanted a moment to myself. My second trip to the Camino, in May 2016, surprised me, as it was quite different from my first, being full of conversation and community, not the solitary adventure I expected it to be.

Guiding a small group of women as part of a fundraiser for United Planet, where I was a board member, I was surprised to never be alone on my second Camino. Having expected it to be similar to my first experience, I had looked forward to some downtime to reflect on what had transpired since my first pilgrimage: seventeen years of marriage, six moves in fourteen years, two daughters, one mother free of cancer, building the team that would unite and transform high-potential leadership development at Microsoft, my exit from a corporate role, and the launch of my own leadership consulting firm.

"I'll wait for you," he responded. "Seriously?" I thought as I instantaneously understood, "Ahh, it's not that kind of Camino."

I adjusted my boot and walked over to my new friend. We began to walk. "I'm John." "Shannon," I replied, "What calls you to the Camino, John?"

"Oh, what an unusual question," he stammered. "Most people ask where you're from."

I chuckled, "I'm not most people." And then, I asked again, softly, sensing the need for sensitivity, "What called you to the Camino, John?"

He cleared his throat, "Well, there were supposed to be six of us, but now there are five. My wife passed away last month." Bam! If I had any doubt from the past two days, it was now crystal clear. This Camino was not about being alone and individual reflection. This Camino was about being of service. For the next two hours, I walked with John and listened to the story of his life, his wife's battle with cancer, her remission, their group's other walks and plans for the Camino, his wife's recurrence of cancer, and her recent passing.

"Our friends have been wonderful and were willing to postpone the trip, but I knew that she would still want us to go. But sometimes it's hard to be with them all of the time. It's a constant reminder, and they are always concerned. I decided to take a bit of a break from it before I saw you."

John needed a stranger to talk to, someone who would listen, but have less attachment. His story touched me; I remembered how I felt on my first Camino. I listened, empathized, and wished him "Buen Camino" with a big hug when we parted ways. "It will get better," I said.

The remainder of the Camino was much the same: meeting new people, asking what called them to the Camino, listening with compassion to what they said and what they didn't say, and responding with empathy. If the Camino is a metaphor for life, my life had changed, and for the better. I was no longer journeying alone; I was consciously walking step by step along a well-used path, among a community of pilgrims, but this time, I understood my role: I was to be of service.

As I stated in the introduction, in the years since the Camino, it has become increasingly apparent to me that my life has been, and is, about being of service. I am a messenger of hope, an agent of transformation, a guardian of the innocent, a mother to the Lovelies, and guide for *WE the Change*.

Messenger of Hope: Anything is possible. The transformation in my life situation, alone, tends to be one that gives hope to others in similar situations. Because I choose to share my story and share the lessons I've learned, others have called me a messenger.

Agent of Transformation: I'm not satisfied with "what ifs" that lead to "only ifs," and you shouldn't be either. I am a student of transformational change. Not only have I experienced it personally but I have also studied it and dedicated my work to helping others achieve it—individually, with their teams, and with their organizations.

Guardian of the Innocent: My vision is to help, in some small way, shape, or form, to eradicate poverty and to help others find their voice. From children born into challenging circumstances to leaders working to launch Big Ideas and create New Realities, we all begin in the stage of Innocence along our individual hero's journey.

Mother to the Lovelies: Years ago, I nicknamed my daughters, "the Lovelies." Little did I know that I would come to think of my young female clients and others who were working to uplift their lives as belonging to this group as well, but I did. And I find incredible satisfaction, just as any proud mama would, when they achieve success. Literally and figuratively, I am a mother to my Lovelies.

Guide for WE the Change: The power of relationships has become more and more meaningful as I journey through life. None of us go it alone, even when we think we do. In becoming conscious of our connections to each other, the power of our collective spirits can rise. We must not only "be the change" but also WE the Change. Together, not separately, we will launch the Big Ideas and create the New Realities that are truly transformational. I am humbled to act as a guide along this path in the quest for greater collective consciousness and manifestation.

With these many dimensions of my purpose, I am honored to work collectively with you to more effectively build a community of Supporters who enable each other to launch Big Ideas and create New Realities. With the lessons of the Camino as our roadmap, we can *WE the Change* to realize our individual and collective dreams. And, as we lift our spirits together, we will also transform our communities.

¡Buen Camino!

Shannon Wallis
June 28, 2019
Santiago de Compostela, Spain

The adventure begins. Shannon and Susan
at the Madrid train station.

Shannon and Susan on the Camino.

Shannon walking the pilgrim's path.

At a Camino café, a break for the feet.

Finding the yellow arrows and scallop shells wasn't always easy.

Having pilgrim fun.

Our friend Lori in the wheat fields.

Innovation on the Camino.

Close to Santiago.

Standing at the original pilgrims' hospital in Santiago.

Count your blessings, not your blisters! Celebrating
in front of the Cathedral de Santiago!

¡Buen Camino!

PART TWO

WE THE CHANGE: LAUNCHING BIG IDEAS AND CREATING NEW REALITIES WORKBOOK

"When we seek connection, we restore the world to wholeness. Our seemingly separate lives become meaningful as we discover how truly necessary we are to each other."
— Margaret Wheatley

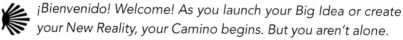 *¡Bienvenido! Welcome! As you launch your Big Idea or create your New Reality, your Camino begins. But you aren't alone. I am with you in spirit to guide your first steps along your path. Each chapter of the story has an accompanying chapter in the workbook, with a set of coaching exercises denoted by the Camino scallop shell. They are included to bring the lesson to life and are meant to encourage you and remove the blockages you encounter. Some of the activities will resonate with you; others may not. Use what works for you. Don't feel obligated to complete all activities. Find the ones that ring true for you, and work with them.*

With that in mind, I will give you some nudges along the path regarding my favorite activities that I know require more work and may not be as energizing to some. When we get to those tools, I'll invite you to experiment with them, even if they seem foreign to you. I've included them because I am passionate about them and the difference they can make in achieving your goals. Whether you live in the business world like I do, the art world like my mother, or another one, if you have found this book, these tools are for you.

Now, my friend, let's get started. ¡Buen Camino!

ONE
THE CALL 🐚

LESSON ONE
Anything Is Possible If You Just Say Yes

Have you ever had an idea you sensed you could, or should, bring to life, but you ignored it? The desire gnawed at you a bit, but eventually it subsided. Several months later, maybe even a year, you saw *your idea* in the world. Someone else had *your idea* too, and she had executed it. If you haven't had this experience yet, maybe it is time to pay a little more attention. I think the call is a bit like this—a brilliant, individual snowflake of an idea falls ever so slowly from the heavens. For a brief moment we see or know it and are inspired by the beauty. If we grab hold, it will be ours to launch, but if we only admire it, someone else will reach for it instead.

 VAGUE CALLINGS

Write a response to these three questions:

1. What calling are you not paying attention to?

2. What have you been yearning for but can't quite bring yourself to say out loud for fear of how ridiculous it might seem?

3. What have you resisted saying yes to because you have thought that you aren't capable or *enough* to get the job done?

 D x V x F > R

Remember the simple approach of D x V x F > R (Dissatisfaction x Vision x First Steps overcome, or are greater than, Resistance to Change)

1. Define what you want.
2. Understand where you are starting and what might be getting in the way.
3. Take steps to close the gap.

Let's explore DVFR. We all have successes . . . and failures. Sometimes we forget them. From graduating high school, organizing a volunteer event, starting your first job, and getting your first apartment to managing your first project team, starting a family, competing in a triathlon, and launching a new business, you have successfully changed, achieved, and evolved. Think of a goal you successfully completed, then answer:

1. How were you dissatisfied with your current reality at the time? (D)

2. What did you hope to create or achieve? (V)

3. What first steps did you take to start your journey? (F)

Next, think of another idea that you never finished. Which of these was missing or not overly compelling? Answer:

1. Were you actually content with the status quo? (D)

2. Was your vision of the future clear? (V)

3. Did you know how to get started? (F)

NOTICE THE FOLLOWING:

- You have successfully created or changed something in the past. Take pride in that accomplishment. Trust that, if you have done it once, you can do it again. Know that you have done this more than once.
- When you didn't succeed in the past, an element of D, V, or F was missing, wasn't clear or wasn't compelling. Trust that this awareness can lead to different actions and outcomes next time.

TWO
VISION

LESSON TWO
Know Where You Are Going

Vision. It's what you want to create. Do you know what yours is? Can you tell others in a clear and concise way? Don't be dismayed if the answers are "No." Many of my clients struggle with vision and need encouragement to discover it.

The next two exercises remind you of what you truly *love*. When I was a small child, I wanted to be a ballerina, an actress, and the first female president of the United States. When I reflect on these roles, I see commonality in some of my work today. I still love to perform for a crowd. Put me on center stage and I normally shine. Public speaking is my favorite hobby. I love to share my ideas and others' ideas with an audience. And, I have to admit, I enjoy leading. I like to point to a destination and inspire people to move in that direction with me. I did not end up in any of the three roles I specifically dreamed of, but the essence of each is a part of what I love in my career today.

Time to encourage your creativity.

 POSSIBLE FUTURES

Start by remembering what you have loved and dreamed of.

    1. When I was a child, I dreamed I would grow up to be . . .

    2. When I was a teenager, my fantasies of what I wanted to do in my life were . . .

    3. Reflect:

        ▪ How does your life now (personal and career) compare with your childhood desires?

        ▪ What is the essence of your dreams for yourself?

- How do they or could they become real in your life today?

 MAGIC WAND

If you had a magic wand and could become anyone or do anything, what would it be? The first woman to walk on Mars? A world-famous gospel singer? A scientist who cures cancer? Let your imagination run wild! Don't censor. Nothing is too silly. Just have fun.

Reflect on your answers—or even on the difficulty of answering the questions. Ask yourself: Why did I want to be a _____? What is the essence of that role that truly appealed to me? What did I think I would get out of it? What part appealed to my soul?

Finally, if all else fails, I try this last exercise.

 I WANT TO WANT TO . . .

Imagine you know something you should want. For example, shouldn't everyone want to feel vital, healthy, energized? So, shouldn't they also want to exercise? Not me. It all sounds good, but I don't act on it. In fact, when I first started to focus on my vitality and well-being, I had no desire to eat healthy or exercise. True . . . and I am married to a marine. Instead, I started with, "I *want to* want to live a vital and healthy life filled with energy." I realize that this may sound a bit odd. Still, my idea of what I would have to do, such as exercise and eat healthier foods, got in my way of truly wanting it.

Saying *"I want to want to* _____ (have a more interesting life, feel better about my body, start a new project, etc.)*"* allows me to acknowledge both my resistance to the goal and that it is good for me to have the goal. As crazy as it might sound, I have shared my *I want to want to* exercise with many friends and clients. We all have a good laugh because, while it sounds a bit pathetic, it works. So, who cares what works, as long as it does work?

What do you *want* to want?

 ## WRITE YOUR VISION

Now the time has come to claim what you want. It's the real reason you are here, isn't it? You are reading a book about launching Big Ideas or creating New Realities.

What is it? Don't just think it . . . Write it down. Yes, right here. Go for it.

Now, read your vision out loud to yourself. Notice and replace any language that might be related to "No," is negative, or is about loss. Replace it with a positive statement. For example, "I want the discord in my community to stop" could be reframed as "I want to promote more harmony and understanding in my community." Or, "I don't want to live paycheck to paycheck" could become "I want to be able to support myself in a way that I can feel financially safe and supported." Revise your vision here.

Still find this a bit challenging? Then, challenge your vision by asking a series of questions to discover what you really want.

 CHALLENGE YOUR VISION

Original Vision: *I want to lose weight.*

Next, ask these questions:

Why? *I feel sluggish.*

What is "sluggish"? *I'm tired. My clothes don't fit me well. I don't feel confident in my body.*

What do you really want to happen? *I want to feel better. I want to feel healthy and fit. I want to look better in my clothes.*

Revised Vision: *I want to feel healthy, have more energy, and look good in my clothes.*

Original Vision:

- Why do you want it?

- Why do you want that?

- What do you really want to happen?

THREE
DISSATISFACTION 🐚

> *"You have to go through the falling down in order to learn to walk. It helps to know that you can survive it. That's an education in itself."*
> — Carol Burnett

LESSON THREE
Know What You Are Leaving Behind

If you came to this book with a great idea but lacking sufficient dissatisfaction, we'll work together to help you find it. The easiest way to start is with the most direct question.

What is getting in your way?

As I indicated in the Camino story, when I started writing this book two years ago, I lacked dissatisfaction. I thought my vision would be compelling enough to create the dissatisfaction needed. But it wasn't. Instead, I procrastinated and procrastinated. I built the table of contents. I thought of the research I needed to do. I thought of the models and exercises I'd like to incorporate. I did a lot of thinking, but I didn't write. I thought I could willpower my way to complete it.

In my case, I needed to ask myself not only the first question but the second question as well:

What is really getting in your way?

WHAT IS GETTING IN YOUR WAY?

It's a simple, direct, and important question. Still, it took me years in my coaching work to discover it. I wandered around with other questions, trying to pin down the barriers that were getting in the way of my clients accomplishing their goals. Those questions elicited interesting responses but weren't as focused and wasted time. I have been amazed by how quickly people zero in on the most important obstacles that were impeding progress when asked this one question.

What is getting in your way . . . of achieving your goal, realizing your vision, launching your Big Idea, creating your New Reality?

If this isn't sufficient to generate the dissatisfaction required to overcome resistance, try the next one.

WHAT IS REALLY GETTING IN YOUR WAY?

If you have tried to launch your Big Idea or create your New Reality multiple times *or* the direct approach left you with an insufficient level of dissatisfaction, it's time to dig for buried treasure. The next set of questions will act as your pickaxe, shovel, and dynamite.

Based on the work of Robert Kegan and Lisa Lahey,[22] *What Is REALLY Getting in Your Way?* is my most revealing, mind-shifting exercise for understanding your barriers.

To understand it better, let's start with my example from Chapter Three.

What is your Big Idea or New Reality that you are trying to bring to life?

> *Write a book.*

1. What actions could help you to achieve your goal? List them here:

   a. *Write every day, get a coach, prioritize my time.*

2. What one action in (a), if you did it, might be a game changer in achieving your goal?

   b. *Prioritize my time.*

   (If you aren't sure what actions could help you, ask your closest friends and family. They will have some good ideas. My husband told me right away, "Stop doing so much." Next, how important is this to you? On a scale of 1 to 5, where 1 is "Not at all" and 5 is "Super important," how important is (b) to you? It should be a 4 or 5.)

3. Next, what other actions do you take that get in the way of taking that one action (b)?

   c. *Working, volunteering in my community, spending time with my family, cleaning my kitchen.*

4. Of the actions in (c), which one would be best to explore further? (Use your intuition.)

   d. *Cleaning my kitchen.*

To be clear, your actions indicate that you have decided to *(d) clean your kitchen* instead of *(b) prioritize your time* in order to write a book.

   5. Imagine you start (b) and stop doing (d), what do you fear might happen?

      e. You might see my messy kitchen.

   6. If (e) happens, then what do you fear might happen?

      f. You might think I'm really disorganized.

   7. If (f) happens, then what do you fear might happen?

      g. You might think I'm not competent and my advice is worthless.

   8. If (g) happens, then what do you fear might happen?

      h. You might not hire me or might tell others not to hire me.

   9. And then . . . ?

      i. I will lose my business, and I won't be able to support my family . . .

Found it! The treasure! You might call it your Dreaded Assumption.

   10. What do you feel right now, and where do you feel it in your body?

      j. Deflation, anxiety, fear—in my heart.

   11. Do you remember or have a sense of when you first started thinking this way?

      k. Yes, it started years ago . . .

12. Write your Dreaded Assumption down at this point.

l. I fear that, if I start to prioritize my time instead of cleaning my kitchen, you will think I'm incompetent/not good enough and I won't be able to support my family.

Now we know why I was procrastinating so much. I was warding off certain doom.

Your turn...

What is your Big Idea or New Reality that you are trying to bring to life?

1. What actions could help you to achieve your goal? List them here:

    a.

2. What one action in (a), if you did it, might be a game changer in achieving your goal?

    b.

On a scale of 1 to 5, where 1 is "Not at all" and 5 is "Super important," how important is (b) to you? It should be a 4 or 5.

3. Next, what other actions do you take that get in the way of taking that one action (b)?

c.

4. Of the actions in (c), which one would be best to explore further? (Use your intuition.)

d.

To be clear, your actions indicate that you have decided to

(d)_____

instead of (b)_____

5. Imagine you start (b) and stop doing (d), what do you fear might happen?

e.

6. If (e) happens, then what do you fear might happen?

f.

7. If (f) happens, then what do you fear might happen?

g.

8. If (g) happens, then what do you fear might happen?

h.

9. And then . . . ?

i.

Found it! The treasure! You might call it your Dreaded Assumption.

10. What do you feel right now, and where do you feel it in your body?

11. Do you remember or have a sense of when you first started thinking this way?

12. Write your Dreaded Assumption down at this point.

I fear that, if I start to _____

instead of _____,

then _____ will happen.

Living with this unconscious fear, is it any surprise you aren't working diligently to launch your Big Idea or create your New Reality?

Surfacing your Dreaded Assumption does not mean it is false. It means it can be tested. So, ask yourself, "Is it true?" Even if some truth exists, is it *always* true? Or is it false? Are there places or times it is less true than others? While, for some reason, it has been sitting in your subconscious for a while, this doesn't necessarily make it true today. You are a different person now than the one who originated it. The event or series of events triggering it may not even feel relevant anymore, but the Dreaded Assumption doesn't know it's time to let go of the chokehold. Will the world truly fall apart if you take a new action or eliminate other actions in the effort to achieve your goal?

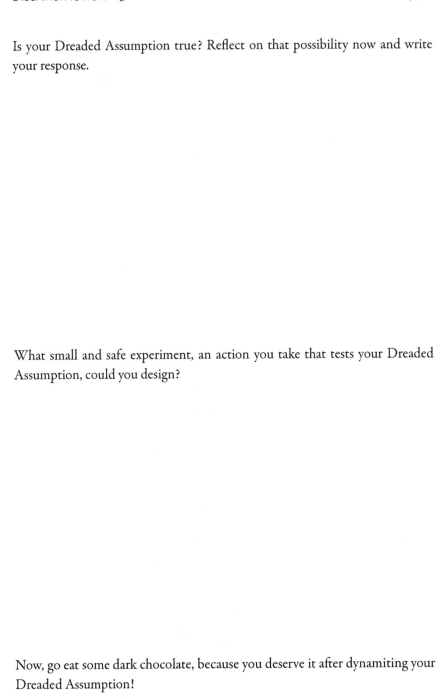

Is your Dreaded Assumption true? Reflect on that possibility now and write your response.

What small and safe experiment, an action you take that tests your Dreaded Assumption, could you design?

Now, go eat some dark chocolate, because you deserve it after dynamiting your Dreaded Assumption!

FOUR
FIRST STEPS 🐚

"We don't accomplish anything in this world alone . . . and whatever happens is the result of the whole tapestry of one's life and all the weavings of individual threads from one to another that creates something."
— Sandra Day O'Connor

LESSON FOUR
Engage Your Supporters

To *WE the Change*, you must involve others. To launch a Big Idea or create a New Reality by yourself is hard. In the business world, no one truly works alone, and collaboration is necessary to launch new ideas. But even when I think of my mom creating a piece of art, which could seem like a solitary and individual effort, she had Supporters who collaborated with her to make it happen. Her kids pitched in and did the laundry or cooked dinner so she could finish her work. Friends helped with carpooling. She wasn't working alone. Her collaboration was different but still present. Knowing who she could rely on was essential to her ability to work.

Exploring who your Supporters are, as well as your Opposers, in advance of it becoming critical, can be the difference between success and failure. In fact, it is so important that I ALWAYS start with this exercise as my First Step after creating Vision and surfacing Dissatisfaction. With that said, this is a series of exercises I mentioned earlier—one where I'll nudge you to complete it, even if you aren't interested. It might take a little bit of time, but here goes...Nudge, nudge.

IDENTIFY AND ENGAGE YOUR SUPPORTERS

In this next set of exercises, you will identify your stakeholders, understand them better, and consider ways to engage them. It can be completed as a simple mental activity or a much more robust, written exploration. Take as much or as little time as you want.

Complete this exercise step by step. It is pretty simple when broken down into baby steps.

Steps are indicated in order for a reason. I think all are relevant and equally important. However, if you only complete Step 1, you are further ahead than most who never do when they launch a Big Idea or create a New Reality.

At a high level, you will:

> **Step 1:** Identify your stakeholders—those who have a stake in the outcome with respect to your Big Idea or New Reality.

> **Step 2:** Determine their level of enthusiasm for your project—friend or foe? Formally known as Supporter, Opposer, Follower (neutral), or Unknown.

> **Step 3:** Engage your Supporters and Opposers.

> **Step 4:** Map their level of power and influence and the degree of cooperation from them required to complete your project.

Step 5: Prioritize and closely manage stakeholders who have high levels of power and influence and whose cooperation is necessary.

STEP 1: IDENTIFY YOUR STAKEHOLDERS AND THEIR PERSPECTIVES.

Identify who might have a stake in the outcome or be affected by your Big Idea or New Reality.

Create a list of stakeholders.

1. Include anyone in a decision-making (or management) role who is impacted by the outcome.

2. Label each stakeholder with a short name or number.

STEP 2: DETERMINE YOUR STAKEHOLDERS' LEVEL OF ENTHUSIASM FOR YOUR PROJECT.

Code your stakeholders by their level of enthusiasm.

Place a colored dot next to each stakeholder to indicate the perspective the stakeholder holds with respect to the project.

> **Green = Supporters.** Positive stakeholders who enthusiastically embrace the project and can act as advocates.

> **Red = Opposers.** Negative stakeholders who do not embrace the project and may actively work to block your project.

> **Blue = Followers.** Neutral stakeholders who are not likely to advocate or block your project but will most likely follow as you move forward.

> **Yellow = Unknown.** Stakeholders whose perspective is unknown. Watch carefully for signs of perspective if these individuals have a high level of power and influence as indicated in Step 4.

STEP 3: ENGAGE YOUR SUPPORTERS AND OPPOSERS.

Engage your Supporters to help you create momentum and overcome obstacles.

Ask your Supporters to speak to stakeholders who may be Followers or Opposers, if you think the Supporter can influence them.* Be clear about the messages you'd like them to deliver, because sharing incorrect information can do more harm than good.

1. Which Supporters would you like to speak to which Followers or Opposers?

2. What messages would you like your Supporters to deliver?

* I call this concept *chains of influence*, using the support of one stakeholder to influence the perspective of another. Kids are experts at this. When my daughters want to watch a movie or series that I think is questionable, they will engage someone else who could persuade me. My youngest will start by referring me to the rating from CommonSenseMedia.org, if it is favorable. If she doesn't think that looks good and knows my sister has allowed my niece to watch it, she asks my sister to tell me her rationale for allowing it. Because I value my sister's perspective, I'll consider it, and my daughters are more likely to get what they want.

3. Meet with your Opposers to understand their concerns.

Opposers are the best source of concerns that may limit your progress. Schedule time to ask questions to better understand their reservations in order to mitigate them. Questions to ask:

- What concerns do you have?

- What gets in your way of supporting the Big Idea or New Reality?

▪ Will you actively block or oppose my moving forward? If so, why?

▪ What do you need included or considered to make this work?

Planning appropriate communication strategies to both deliver the ideal messages and surface barriers is explored more fully in Chapter Seven.

Okay, this is where it gets fun. Continue to Steps 4 and 5 to ensure greater success with your stakeholders. Creating a Stakeholder Prioritization Grid enables you to identify and understand your stakeholders even more. It's a bit like playing a game. Admittedly, the word *grid* could be a turnoff for some. If you are a transformational change geek like me, you will dig it. If it doesn't seem like a step for you, turn it into a more creative one. Put some butcher block paper up on a wall, get your colored markers, make some paper doll faces. (Why not? When was the last time you did that?) The Scarecrow, Tinman, and Cowardly Lion are your Supporters, and Witches are your Opposers. Or try Dove dark chocolate wrappers versus cough drop wrappers. (It should be pretty clear by now which one would be the Supporter.) You get the idea. Make it work for you. Label them with the names of your Supporters and Opposers.

STEP 4: PRIORITIZE YOUR STAKEHOLDERS IN THE GRID.

Prioritize stakeholders according to the level of cooperation you need from them and the level of power and influence they might have over your idea.

Stakeholder Prioritization Grid

High ↑		
	Consult	Engage
Power and Influence Medium		
	Observe	Inform
Low		
	Unnecessary	Desirable	Necessary

Required Cooperation

Look at the Stakeholder Prioritization Grid:[23]

1. Assess the level of Power and Influence and Required Cooperation for each stakeholder:

   - Level of **Power and Influence** = the stakeholder's ability to influence the outcome (i.e., Low, Medium, or High).

   - Level of **Required Cooperation** = the degree to which the stakeholder's cooperation is required (i.e., Unnecessary, Desirable, or Necessary).

2. Place them on the grid, based on your assessment:

Any stakeholder whose cooperation is necessary to your success and holds a high degree of power and influence over your ability to achieve it is placed in the upper right quadrant, **Engage**. These are the people you are looking for. Whether they are Supporters or Opposers, you need to engage and pay close attention to them throughout your project.

Other quadrants for the stakeholders include:

- **Consult** (high power and influence, unnecessary cooperation): Connect with these stakeholders on occasion to gather information to input and support your project. To avoid boredom or irritation, don't over-communicate.

- **Inform** (low power and influence, necessary cooperation): Regularly inform these stakeholders throughout the project so no major issues arise. They are often helpful in providing support for tasks as project milestones are completed.

- **Observe** (low power and influence, unnecessary cooperation): Communicate as needed, but not excessively.

Finally, add the color that indicates their level of enthusiasm, as indicated in Step 2.

STEP 5: ENGAGE—QUESTIONS TO ASK.

Making the effort to understand *all* stakeholders is useful. And it is important to prioritize those in the upper right quadrant. Pay special attention to them (i.e., Engage). Maximize your effort to fully engage them and create buy-in. Consider the following:

- How they feel about and react to your Big Idea or New Reality project.
- Best ways to engage them in it.
- Best means to communicate with them.

Questions that can help you better understand your stakeholders include:

Reaction to Change:

1. What emotional or financial interest do they have in the outcome of your work? Is it positive or negative?

2. What is their current opinion of your work? Is it based on good information?

3. If they are not positive, what gets in their way of supporting it? How could you address this concern?

4. Who else might be influenced by their opinions? Do these people become stakeholders in their own right?

Engagement:

1. What motivates your stakeholders most of all?

2. Who influences their opinions generally, and who influences their opinion of you? Do some of these influencers, therefore, become important stakeholders in their own right?

3. How can you leverage influencers who are Supporters to overcome the obstacles surfaced by the Opposers?

4. If you don't think you will be able to bring them around, how will you manage their opposition?

Communication:

1. What information do they want from you?

2. How often do they require information from you?

3. How do they want to receive information from you? (Consider in person, email, video message, and text.)

4. What is the best way of communicating your message to them? (Consider narrative/storytelling, bullet points, graphs, and data.)

FIVE
THE RIGHT GEAR 🐚

*"Close some doors. Not because of pride, incapacity or arrogance,
but simply because they no longer lead somewhere."*
— Paulo Coelho

LESSON FIVE
Pack Light

Have you ever heard, "What got you here won't get you there"?[24] The skills,
strengths, and capabilities that have enabled your success so far might not all be
useful on this Camino. To get to your destination, you must often discard some
of the approaches, assumptions, and beliefs that made you successful in the past.
By letting go of them, you create space to build new skills, strengths, and capabilities that give you a higher chance of success.

You'll look at what you need to let go of through a few simple questions.

🐚 IT COULD BE EASIER

Just as my coach in my Camino story challenged my beliefs about what made me successful, I will challenge yours. Answer these questions:

1. What do you believe to be true about how you achieve success in the world?

   ▪ When did you form these beliefs?

   ▪ What becomes possible for you if you let go of these beliefs?

2. Think about a time when you were completely certain about an idea and were proven to be completely wrong?

- Why were you wrong?

- How did you discover your error?

3. Did you ever misjudge someone?

- Have you ever been misjudged?

- How are you misjudging yourself now?

4. How old were you when you decided who you are?

- What belief about yourself do you sense no longer serves you?

- What beliefs about yourself might you need to adopt or accept?

5. What belief are you holding about how you must approach your current project that may not be true?

- Why do you think that?

- How could you test it?

SIX
DECISIONS 🐚

"Throughout the course of our lives, events occur that take us in new directions. Sometimes our life changes as the result of deliberate decisions we make."
— Barbara Bernard, *Birthdays of the Soul*

LESSON SIX
Commit to Going and Go!

If you are approaching your New Reality step by step, you might be in the same place I found myself, saying, "I've examined my Dissatisfaction. I've created a detailed picture of my Vision, and I've planned my First Steps. I am ready to begin . . ." You are seemingly ready to jump off the diving board, only to have your Inner Critic hiss, "What are you thinking? You don't know what you're doing. Who are you to set forth on this lofty adventure?"

Soft or loud, she is in your head, ready to point out each and every way that you are unworthy and destined to fail.

At this point on your Camino, you need special tools to recommit to your vision.

CRITIC'S JOURNAL[25]

> *"The Critic's Journal is a place to give voice to the Voices in your*
> *head that will undermine and destroy your creative self if you do*
> *not acknowledge them. It's like a child locked in the bathroom,*
> *screaming and trying to kick the door down. You simply can't*
> *ignore the child. You open the door, let her out, let him cry and*
> *rant a bit, and soon enough they will be playing quietly in the*
> *corner and you can get back to work. The Critic's Journal is a*
> *transformational tool. As simple as it appears, it is powerful.*
> *Because it's the place where you meet yourself, all your selves,*
> *all the parts of you that are fighting to stop you from expressing*
> *or discovering your vision. You must be willing to acknowledge*
> *these seemingly destructive voices—and you must be willing to*
> *give them the space to rant and rave."* — Marcia Zina Mager

Select a special journal which will become your Critic's Journal for this purpose. In this journal, with your trusty sword/pen, unleash her. Write anything that comes to mind. From the mundane thoughts to the nasty barbs, write them down. Write until you feel more aware of what is going on in your mind and body, whether it is negative or positive. Write until you feel calmer and clear-minded. Write until you have nothing left to say on the topic for the moment. Then, and only then, return to your Big Idea or New Reality.

Need extra support? Move onto the next tool.

MEDITATION: WHO ARE YOU NOT TO BE?

In the words of Marianne Williamson, "Who am I to be brilliant, gorgeous, talented, fabulous? Actually, who are you *not* to be?" Your Inner Critic's voice asks the first question, sowing doubt to sabotage your potential. Your *Inner Creator's* voice asks the second question, raising awareness that you are a child of God, destined to realize it.

In a quiet place, read Marianne Williamson's call to your soul.[26] Shut your eyes for one minute and think of a beautiful white light before you and ask the light, "Who is called to launch this idea . . . ? If I don't launch it, who will . . . ?"

> *"Our deepest fear is not that we are inadequate. Our deepest fear is that we are powerful beyond measure. It is our light, not our darkness that most frightens us. We ask ourselves, Who am I to be brilliant, gorgeous, talented, fabulous? Actually, who are you not to be? You are a child of God. Your playing small does not serve the world. There is nothing enlightened about shrinking so that other people won't feel insecure around you. We are all meant to shine, as children do. We were born to make manifest the glory of God that is within us. It's not just in some of us; it's in everyone. And as we let our own light shine, we unconsciously give other people permission to do the same. As we are liberated from our own fear, our presence automatically liberates others."*
> — Marianne Williamson

After your meditation, revisit your D, V, and F. Remind yourself, what inspired you in the first place? Where does your desire come from?

 ## 10 / 10 / 10[27]

Think of the Big Idea or New Reality you want to create. Consider stopping, quitting, postponing, or whatever you want to call it. Next, envision yourself in three different time periods from now: ten minutes, ten months, and ten years.

Ask yourself: If I don't follow through on my idea, what are the consequences and how will I feel . . .

- Ten minutes from now?

- Ten months from now?

- Ten years from now?

- What do you discover?

- What will you do next as a result of your discovery?

SEVEN
GETTING THERE TOGETHER 🐚

"Find the courage to ask questions and to express what you really want. Communicate with others as clearly as you can to avoid misunderstandings, sadness and drama." — Don Miguel Ruiz, *The Four Agreements*

LESSON SEVEN
Say What Needs to Be Said

At some point, you will need to improve communication to launch your Big Idea or create your New Reality. It is inevitable. Even the best communicators are surprised by how often they must communicate the same message to their intended audience. Becoming familiar with the two tools presented in this section can support your forward momentum. If they aren't relevant now, book-mark them for the future.

The foundation of better communication starts with these four principles:
1. **Be present.**
2. **Listen.**
3. **Ask questions.**
4. **Express yourself.**

Notice the order. Communication with others begins with being present. It is easy to *appear* present and not as easy to *be* present. Listening is next. A desire to truly listen opens the channel of communication so it can become a two-way dialogue. Asking questions follows and demonstrates your openness to learn and consider new information and perspectives. Finally, expressing yourself intentionally comes last. This can be especially hard for extroverts who like to think out loud. Once you've demonstrated the first three to the receiver of your message, they are more likely to be open to the information you want to share.

With this in mind, let's dive into these two tools to improve communication and support you getting there together.

FIVE FATAL FLAWS OF COMMUNICATION

You've started to tell people about your plans to launch your Big Idea or create your New Reality. You want them to understand because you want their help and support. But they don't always seem to understand. Why not? It could be due to one of the Five Fatal Flaws of Communication.[28]

When sharing your good news about launching your Big Idea or creating a New Reality, check:

- **Did they hear it?** The adult attention span may only be eight seconds, shorter than a goldfish's![29] Were they in the room literally or figuratively, making their grocery list in their head while you shared the good news?

- **Did they understand it?** Test their understanding by asking them to explain it to you in their own words.

- **Did they agree with it?** How many times have you participated in the *meeting, after the meeting,* to discuss what really just happened in there.

- **Did they care about it?** How important is the change to their continued success?

- **Will they act on it?** Are they up for the challenge of implementing the steps that will help you move forward?

If the answers to any of these questions is "No," explore where the confusion or resistance is coming from. This may lead to engaging in a Productive Dialogue.

PRODUCTIVE DIALOGUE

I can't think of a client who hasn't said to me at some point, "I just don't know how to bring it up," or "I don't know how to talk to her." Difficult conversations between two or more people where the conflict exists and the stakes feel high are a fact of life. While my clients most often raise such conversations from their professional settings, all of them say that this tool helps them most with friends and family.

Productive Dialogue is the transformation of the difficult conversation. It is the exchange of information, plus *why we care* about it, so that collaborative behavior can achieve the desired goal. With practice, it ensures that a positive outcome is reached without the dialogue escalating. What constitutes a difficult conversation is different for people. In the business environment, giving constructive/negative feedback to a direct report, peer, or manager is the most common difficult conversation raised by my clients. I've also heard:

- Talking to my partner about money.
- Discussing *my* parenting style with my parents.
- Getting funding or resources for a project.

Productive Dialogue has four parts that I mentioned briefly in my Camino narrative. Context, Consent, Content, and Conclusion—the four Cs.[30] And you've already been practicing with it since you started the workbook, because

Productive Dialogue, in this case, is actually VxDxF. This equation is why you get a different outcome.

Roll up your sleeves. Let's figure this out together. I've placed an asterisk (*) in the locations that make Productive Dialogue different from and more useful than a difficult conversation.

- **Context*** is what you really want, framed in the positive, NOT what you are trying to eliminate.
- **Consent*** is the affirmation to dialogue that you seek when you invite the other person to the conversation.
- **Content*** is the sharing of authentic information, data, thoughts, and feelings between both parties in order to develop a deeper understanding of the issue at hand. Sharing has two pieces; learning from the other person *and then* sharing your own thoughts.
- **Conclusion** is the resolution, or next steps, to which you both agree at the end of the conversation.

PRODUCTIVE DIALOGUE = VxDxF

CONTEXT ➟ CONSENT ➟ CONTENT ➟ CONCLUSION

VISION ✖ DISSATISFACTION ✖ FIRST STEPS

In difficult conversations, you typically launch into your view of the Content and start with what the other party is not doing well. In Productive Dialogue, Context and Consent create greater psychological safety to begin the conversation: Context focuses on a positive outcome to create versus a negative one to eliminate; Consent happens in the rational part of your brain, not in the primitive amygdala. (I loosely include Consent in Vision because, in theory, a person is also agreeing to the Context statement, thus creating a shared vision for the conversation participants.) Asking for the other person's perspective before sharing your own Content demonstrates your desire to truly learn and creates greater understanding. These three components are critical to creating truly Productive Dialogue.

If you were to think of it visually, you would see a loop where, in the upper right, **Context** leads to affirmative **Consent**, which enables the speakers to enter into the **Content** of the difficult conversation, which eventually leads to a more useful **Conclusion**, which creates trust to raise the **Context** for the next difficult conversation.

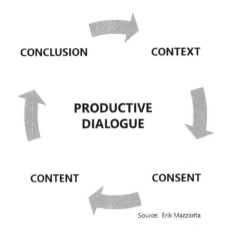

CONCLUSION   CONTEXT

**PRODUCTIVE
DIALOGUE**

CONTENT   CONSENT

Source: Erik Mazziotta

To prepare for a Productive Dialogue, I recommend this three-step approach:

- **Step 1:** Create your opening statements or questions for Context, Consent, Content, and Conclusion.
- **Step 2:** Practice with a friend.
- **Step 3:** Iterate with feedback.

In Chapter Seven, I refer to a conversation I had with Susan. To get started here, I'll share another example which comes up in relationships—balance in who is doing the work. While you may live alone now, you haven't always done so, and living with other people tends to create this issue. Division of labor is never perfectly fair.

> We had just had a party at our home, my husband was downstairs watching soccer, I was in the kitchen cleaning up and washing dishes, and I was pissed. In my head, I was zipping through my *Greatest Hits* album, called *How He's Wronged Me* (must be a country album). You may know some of the tunes: "Do You Even Notice When I'm Not With You?" "What Do You Think I'm Doing Now?" "I Work Too, Buddy!" "Why Is Cleaning Exclusively My Job? Because I'm a Woman . . . ?"

Instead of launching into the *Greatest Hits*, which is what I have often done and where most difficult conversations begin, I paused and reflected. What was true in this situation? What do I really want? I thought about what I wanted from three perspectives: the outcome, the relationship, and the values. A summary of our conversation from my side follows:

It's important to me that we are a team and that our girls see us being a team. For me, teamwork looks like us working together to achieve a result.	**Context**
When could we talk about that?	**Consent**
How do you think we are doing as a team? . . . I'm noticing something a little different. When we have a party, you are great at hosting and entertaining our guests. Before and after the party, I do most of the work. When that happens, I find myself feeling resentful and angry.	**Content**
What do you think we could do together to be more of a team?	**Conclusion**

Until we had that conversation, I think he could sense that I was irritated but wasn't really sure why and didn't want to ask for fear of the difficult conversation that would ensue. After we talked about what teamwork could really look like for us, behaviors changed in both of us. I expressed more of what I wanted, instead of bottling up my resentment, and he treated our parties like any good teammate does: pre-game, game, and post-game.

Now, it's your turn. *Nudge, nudge.*

STEP 1: CREATE YOUR OPENING STATEMENTS OR QUESTIONS

CONTEXT

Identify what is important to you or what you want. What is your shared goal for the outcome, relationship, or personal values?

My Example: *It's important to me that we are a team and that our girls see us being a team. For me, teamwork looks like us working together to achieve a result.*

- **Outcome:** *I want a clean kitchen, and I want help cleaning the kitchen.*
- **Relationship:** *I want us to be a team.*
- **Personal Values:** *I want our daughters to see that cleaning the kitchen isn't exclusively a woman's job; it's everyone's job.*

Other Examples:

- **Outcome:** *I'd like to work with you to get our project back on track to its original implementation date. I propose that we discuss the problems that are blocking that and figure out some solutions.*
- **Relationship:** *It's important to me to create warm and caring relationships amongst team members so we have each other's backs.*
- **Personal Values:** *It's important to me that we collaborate effectively on this project so we can deliver an exceptional product. I would like to know your thoughts on how to work best together.*

Questions to Consider:

- What outcome do you hope to achieve?

- What do you want to happen or what is important to you? (Does it relate to the results, relationship, or values?)

- What do you think the other party wants to happen or is important to them? (Does it relate to the results, relationship, or values?)

- What do you both want and consider to be important?

CONSENT

Invite the other person to the conversation, creating more psychological safety and willingness. Check that the other person is ready and willing to engage. An invitation creates choice for the other person and helps to reduce the defensive response often observed when you launch into your concerns.

Consider:

- Right time and place.
- Concerns or conflicts that could block being fully open.

My Example:

- *When could we talk about that?*

Other Examples:

- *When is a good time for you to have this conversation (today, this week, etc.)?*
- *How does having this conversation sound to you?*
- *What do you need in order for us to talk about this?*

Questions to Consider:

- When is the right time for you to hold the conversation?

- What will enable you to be present and at your best for the conversation?

CONTENT

Ask about your partner's perspective, then share your own to deepen understanding of the issue at hand with respect to the Context. It consists of observations, information, inferences, assumptions, beliefs, opinions, thoughts, and feelings.

As indicated previously, it is executed in two parts. First, you ask questions to learn how the other party perceives the situation. It may seem counterintuitive but is critical. Launching into your own content or conclusions without first exploring the other person's will most likely put them on the defensive. You think you know what they think, how they perceive the situation, why they are doing or not doing something that gets in the way of achieving the aspiration. You might know some of it. Still, if this is a difficult conversation for you, you don't know all of it. Getting their perspective first helps you to learn what you might be missing about the situation.

My Example:

- *How do you think we are doing as a team? . . . I'm noticing something a little different. When we have a party, you are great at hosting and entertaining our guests. Before and after the party, I do most of the work. When that happens, I find myself feeling resentful and angry.*

Other Examples:

- **Outcome**: *I noticed you missed the last deliverable date.*
- **Relationship**: *I've observed that you haven't stopped by my office lately.*
- **Personal Values**: *The team says you haven't participated in best practice discussions.*

Questions to ask the other person:

- When you consider the goal we share_____
  _____ (Context statement here), how close do you think we are to achieving it on a scale of 1 to 10, where 1 is "Nowhere near it" and 10 is "We have achieved it"?
- What contributes to your rating?
- What information forms your perspective?
- What assumptions have you made or conclusions have you drawn about the situation?

After hearing from the other party, share your thoughts on the matter. Be prepared to speak to the same questions you pose to the other person.

Express your thinking:

- When I consider the goal presented in (Context statement here), I think we're at a 6, because . . .

- I've observed . . . and . . .

- I have assumed . . . and have concluded . . . about the situation.

Don't be surprised if some of your original ideas and statements change based on the comments made by the other person. New information tends to change assumptions.

Questions to Consider:

- What information have you paid closest attention to in this situation?

- What have you observed, inferred, assumed about the situation?

- What have you concluded as a result?

- What information is most relevant to share as you explain your perspective on the issue?

CONCLUSION

Create resolution and establish next steps for action. It might include: agreements as to how to proceed; accountabilities; and specific commitments for action.

My Example:

- *What do you think we could do together to be more of a team?*

Other Examples:

- **Outcome:** *I will contact the sender by end of day Wednesday to check on next steps . . . and send you an email by lunch on Thursday with the status.*
- **Relationship:** *I'll set up some team building and social events for our team to get to know each other better.*
- **Personal Values:** *We agree to meet the first of each month to provide feedback to each other regarding collaboration between each other's departments. We will bring specific examples of any situations that we feel have and have not gone well.*

Questions to Consider:

- What agreement or commitment do you hope to achieve by the end of the conversation?

- What are some appropriate next steps?

PUTTING IT TOGETHER

- My Context statement: I'd like to have a conversation about:

- My Consent question:

- My Content questions:

- My Content expressions:

- My Conclusion question:

🐚 STEP 2: PRACTICE WITH A FRIEND

Find a friend for a practice round. You wouldn't expect to score the winning goal the first time you play soccer: Don't expect to have a Productive Dialogue without some practice. Role-playing enables you to test your approach and messages, get feedback from the *Receiver* on how your messages land, and make adjustments before you engage in the actual conversation. If the stakes are high, it's worth the investment of time. Ask your friend:

- What did you think and feel when I started the conversation?

- What did you think and feel when I asked for your perspective about the situation?

- What did you think and feel when I shared my perspective of the situation?

- What would you recommend I do to make the conversation better?

STEP 3: ITERATE WITH FEEDBACK

Make changes based on what you learn from your role-play experience and try it again with your friend. Keep practicing until it feels *about right*.

- What did you learn?

- What will you do next as a result of your learning?

Communicating clearly to launch your Big Idea or create your New Reality takes patience and practice. I am so passionate about transforming difficult conversations into Productive Dialogue that I've put videos on my website so you can learn more about it. Visit www.wethechange.solutions to access those resources.

EIGHT
VIGILANCE 🐚

> *"These pains you feel are messengers. Listen to them."*
> — Rumi, *The Essential Rumi*

LESSON EIGHT
Seek the Signals and Signposts

How do you know when you are on track or not on track? Whether emotional or intellectual, patterns exist to support your endeavors. You have to become conscious of them in order to learn from them. Then you can leverage them to your advantage. The next four exercises can help you to recognize the patterns. I've also included one, the last one, which you can think of as a best practice, an approach that is considered highly effective. You can try it and revise it as needed, often referred to as adopt or adapt in the consulting world. Use what works and leave the rest.

 "F"ING UP

Knowing how you typically respond to stress, anxiety, and fear is the first step toward seeing the signs. An event triggers an emotion which leads to a physical response of fight, flight, freeze, or flock. Different types of events or triggers may lead to a similar physical response at differing levels of intensity, from mild to extreme, such as irritation to anger.

For one week, journal about what happens when you are under pressure or stress. Notice:

- What was the triggering event?

- When did it occur?

- In what situation/context did it occur?

- What was your "F" tendency:

  □ **Fight:** Did you get busy with activity? Did you start trying to fix something?

  □ **Flight:** Did you retreat from the situation or leave the room? Did you change the subject completely? Did you use strategies to detach from the emotion, such as becoming overly analytical when you tend to be a more emotional person?

  □ **Freeze:** Did your mind go blank? Did you become quiet or shut down? Did you feel immobilized or nothing at all?

  □ **Flock:** Did you look for others to commiserate with? Did you begin to gossip about the problem or people?

- What pattern do you observe in these events?

- What do you learn from them?

PAUSE, REFLECT, AND CHOOSE

When you are triggered and likely to "F" things up: Pause, Reflect, and Choose.

Pause: Take a breath, literally. **Try Four Square Breathing**: Sit straight in your chair with your feet flat on the floor and your hands relaxed in your lap. Close your eyes if you feel safe and comfortable enough to do so. Or pick a spot on a wall or the floor to stare at. Imagine that each four-second step in this exercise is drawing one side of an imaginary square. Close your mouth and breathe in slowly and deeply through your nose, to the count of four. Feel your belly expand as you inhale. Hold your breath for four seconds. You are not trying to deprive your body of oxygen but need to allow a few seconds for the air to fill your lungs. Open your mouth slightly and slowly exhale to a count of four. Hold the exhale to another count of four. As follows:

- Inhale 1, 2, 3, 4 while drawing up from the bottom left to the upper left corner of the square.
- Hold 1, 2, 3, 4 while drawing from the upper left to upper right corner of the square.
- Exhale 1, 2, 3, 4 while drawing from the upper right to the lower right corner of the square.
- Hold 1, 2, 3, 4 while drawing from the lower right to the lower left corner of the square.

Repeat the breathing cycle three or four times to reduce stress and cortisol levels.

Reflect: You are responding to an event based on the assumptions you have made about it. Create at least five more assumptions for the behavior you are noticing.

Example: My boss didn't say hello this morning because . . .

- Initial assumption: *She's mad at me because I missed the deliverable date and turned in my report this morning instead of yesterday.*
- New assumption #1: *She's wondering how she can hold firm with our customer without giving into more demands and expanding the scope of the project.*
- New assumption #2: *She just learned that she has to head the new project and is feeling overwhelmed.*
- New assumption #3: *She had an argument with her daughter on the way to school and is feeling regretful.*
- New assumption #4: *She's thinking about the new car she is going to buy.*

- New assumption #5: *She's thinking about how to get approval for the promotion she promised me last quarter and realizes her time is nearly up.*

Choose: Consider at least two options for how to respond that are different from your typical "F":

- Option 1: Be aware of which way you normally respond: fight, flight, freeze, or flock.
- Option 2: Express and Inquire – Explain the specific behaviors and actions you are noticing and ask your boss what is on her mind and/or how you can help.
- Option 3: Wait and Observe – Don't do anything. Allow your boss to come to you in her own time and observe how she responds to you then.

CONNECT THE DOTS

You can pause in many ways—take a breath, Four Square Breathing, count to ten, go for a walk, listen to calming music, take a bath, have a cup of tea, etc. Use one of your favorites to quiet your mind so you can listen to your inner voice. In the quiet moments, what do you notice?

Journal for ten minutes about when you know your intuition is speaking to you. What is your equivalent of visceral response, rule of threes, and volunteers?

Now try a couple of questions: What's getting in the way of moving forward? What have I learned during this period of inactivity?

 ## STICKY NOTE PLANNING

This exercise comes from my business experience, but I once used it to help a friend who was directing a short film in Madrid. She thought it was amazing and told me I could have a career in Hollywood just building project plans to keep film production on track. I assured her that there were people more skilled at it than I am, but it was flattering that she thought it made such a difference for her project. (And the Oscar for Best Project Plan goes to . . .)

I like to make it fun, so I put a large piece of butcher block or flip chart paper on my wall and use large, 3x3-inch sticky notes. When I don't have wall space, I use 8 ½ x 11-inch paper (A4 paper in Europe) and use smaller 2x2-inch sticky notes. (Yes, I know the dimensions of my sticky notes. We have already established I'm a bit of a geek.)

Once you have your paper, sticky notes, and pens, it is time to practice.

Think of a successful project you were a part of in the past.

1. Writing only one idea per sticky note, what steps did you take to get started? Keep writing one idea per note until you get stuck.
2. When you are stuck, work backwards. Think of the steps you took right before you finished your project. Write them down, one idea per note.
3. When you get stuck again, attach the sticky notes to the wall, window, big piece of butcher block, or flip chart paper. Ideally, attach them to a place that can stay in place for a while.

4. Begin to group and sequence your steps as I shared in my Camino story (a reminder of the chart is included here for ease).

5. Keep working until you have most of the big groups. *These are your milestones.*

6. Notice the groups and the steps. Although the exact words won't be the same for your current project, identify similar steps/sticky notes and place a ✓ on those steps.

7. From here, begin to build a new *Project Plan*. You might want to use a different color note to identify your new project. *I recommend keeping the steps for your completed project intact and writing duplicate notes for the new project.* Sometimes it helps to look at the entire map for the past project.

8. Test your plan. Ask others to look at it, and then add any missing steps based on their experience of completing projects.

Project X: How to Start the Camino

As a reference, the phases of a business project to launch a Big Idea or create a New Reality typically group as follows:

Change Management Project Plan

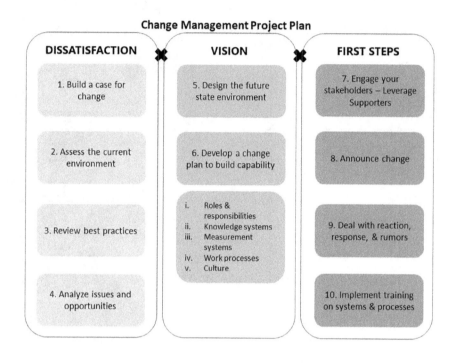

NINE
NO PAIN, NO GAIN 🐚

"Perhaps some of us have to go through dark and devious ways before we can find the river of peace or the highroad to the soul's destination."
— Joseph Campbell, *The Hero With a Thousand Faces*

LESSON NINE

It Wouldn't Be a Pilgrimage If It Weren't Challenging (aka This Is Hard)

"**W**hat have you learned?" is a favorite question of mine, one that's been used multiple times throughout the workbook already. While we can all learn from past successes and failures, I often find myself in the position of helping my clients remember *how* they learn. They tell me how they've never done anything like this before and have no idea how to get started. Really? Are you sure about that? You are constantly adapting from what you have learned. You may not be conscious of it. You will change that here by exploring the Hero's Journey of your past and current experience to identify your own tips and practices that can support you in your current journey.

🐚 A SUCCESSFUL HERO'S JOURNEY

Remember a prior transition, challenge, idea launch, etc. that you experienced and **successfully completed.** We'll call it your Successful Hero's Journey (SHJ).

Complete the following:

- Write a brief description (a couple of sentences) of what happened to launch the last SHJ and how it ended. Be sure to include the results of it in your description.

- How were you in a state of innocence in your life at this time? What felt easy, safe, or at least comfortably familiar?

- What circumstances called you to change? How did you answer the call? Why did you answer it?

- What was your *strange world*? What seemed uncertain, unclear, or especially difficult on this journey? Looking back, what were you being called to surrender?

- Who or what were your Supporters on this particular quest?

- What was the breakthrough for you in that challenge? What did resolution look like?

- What changed because of the completion of your challenge? How were you different? How did you benefit? How did other people benefit?

- If you had to name your myth, what would it be called? "The Story of . . ."

Reading through your responses,

- What contributed to your success?

- What do you learn from your SHJ?

- What tips or practices could you adopt and adapt to support you as you launch your Big Idea or create your New Reality?

YOUR CURRENT HERO'S JOURNEY

Concept adapted from The Path of the Everyday Hero.[31]

Think about the Big Idea you are trying to launch or the New Reality you are currently trying to create. We'll call this your Current Hero's Journey (CHJ). Next, read the instructions below.

Sit comfortably and relax by focusing on your breathing for a few moments. Don't try to breathe differently, just pay attention to your breath, quietly coming into you and then flowing out.

After a few moments, look at the U-curve and think about the CHJ you are experiencing. Where can you be found on the U-curve?

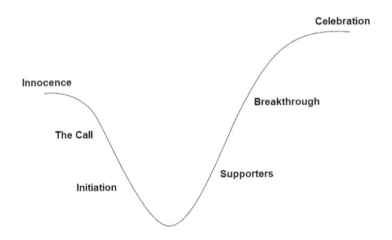

What images or sensations do you have in your body right now? Notice how you feel when you ask yourself that question. Draw a small stick figure on the path, using its position on the U-curve and its body posture to represent where you are now on your journey. Do this without thinking or analyzing. Let your intuition rather than your mind decide how and where to draw the figure.

When you've finished, look at the figure you drew. See if it is positioned in a way to represent where you feel you truly are on this journey of transition. If it needs to be redrawn now that you see it, draw it again.

- What do you learn about how and where you have positioned yourself?

- What do you need to do to support yourself and be at your best while at this stage of your CHJ?

- What will you do next for yourself and to launch your Big Idea or create your New Reality as a result of your learning from both your SHJ and CHJ?

TEN
SURRENDER 🐚

"Perhaps all the dragons in our lives are princesses who are only waiting to see us act, just once, with beauty and courage. Perhaps everything that frightens us is, in its deepest essence, something helpless that wants our love."
— Rainer Maria Rilke, *Letters to a Young Poet*

LESSON TEN
Face Your Dragons

Now that you have a better understanding of what has enabled you to be successful in your own journey, you also need to consider what has prevented success—the dragons. Dragons guard treasure, so learning from failure and success are equally valuable. Both accelerate your ability to launch your Big Idea or create your New Reality.

🦪 GREET YOUR DRAGONS

In Chapter Nine (workbook), you explored a prior Hero's Journey that was successfully completed: your SHJ. This time, you will compare and contrast by exploring the opposite. Consider one of your prior transitions, challenges, idea launches, etc. that stalled or failed. First, write a brief description (just a couple of sentences) of what happened and how it ended. Call this prior Hero's Journey the Unsuccessful Hero's Journey (UHJ), and answer the following questions:

- At what step in the UHJ did you stop?

- What was happening when you stopped?

- What got in your way of success?

- What did you try, without success, to prevent failure?

- In comparing your UHJ to your prior SHJ, what similarities were present? What differences were present?

- What do the similarities suggest about your *go-to strategy*, or standard approach, that served you in the SHJ but overstayed its welcome in the UHJ?

- What do you learn from this comparison? What will you do differently this time as a result?

🐚 DISCOVERING TREASURE

Return to the Successful Hero's Journey, SHJ, you explored in Chapter Nine (workbook).

- What dragon(s) did you face and overcome?

- What did they have to surrender?

- What unique strengths or talents were highlighted or developed?

- Beyond the desire to achieve success, what connects your SHJ and CHJ?

- What becomes possible if you let go of your habitual approach to success to embrace a new way?

- What do you learn and what will you do differently as you launch your Big Idea or create your New Reality?

WE THE CHANGE

I've said it before and I'll say it again. No one truly succeeds alone when they are launching a Big Idea or creating a New Reality. Think back to Chapter Four (workbook) and the Supporters you considered. If you haven't actively engaged them, now is the time to welcome them on your CHJ.

- Who are the stakeholders or resources you could engage at this time?

- Who has offered support or resources you have rejected or postponed?

- What treasure could they contribute to move your project closer to your destination?

- How could you include them now?

- What is the first step you will take to welcome them?

ELEVEN
GRATITUDE

" 'Thank you' is the best prayer that anyone could say . . . Thank you expresses extreme gratitude, humility, understanding."
— Alice Walker

LESSON ELEVEN
Count Your Blessings—Not Your Blisters!

As we come to the end of our journey together, I want you to have a few more tools to help you continue onwards. These tools will support you in the moments when it seems just a little too hard and will enable you to open your ability to innovate, collaborate, and celebrate. While we may be finished in our work together, your Camino continues. Let's ensure it is a good one.

PRACTICE GRATITUDE

Just as some events trigger you negatively, gratitude triggers a positive set of responses in the brain, opening your ability to innovate, collaborate, and celebrate. Try one of these gratitude practices:

- **Carpool Gratitude:** On the mornings I drive the car pool, the five souls in our Honda minivan, including myself, offer up gratitude and blessings. Each person says,

  "I am grateful for

  _____

  (the sun, my home, transportation, a good grade, last night's team win). I send blessings to

  _____

  (those who are homeless, so that they find shelter; my brother, so that he does well on his exams; my aunt, so that her surgery goes well; the teachers, so that they can be patient with their students)." It is heartwarming to hear what each person is grateful for and find yourself grateful for the same once you've been reminded of them.

- **Commuting Gratitude:** If you are on your own, say aloud to yourself at least ten people, objects, moments, or accomplishments that you are grateful for in your life as you commute to work.

- **End-of-Day Gratitude:** At the close of the day, journal about what you were most grateful for in the day's events, maybe a friend's support, a stranger allowing you to go before her in the grocery line, your partner's unprompted foot massage.

- What are you grateful for? Take a moment now to capture it.

- What do you feel after completing the gratitude exercise?

- What are you ready to do next in this state of gratitude?

Hint: Let's innovate, collaborate, and celebrate.

THE MORAL OF THE STORY

I have shared my story, and I have asked you to learn from your own stories. Next, I'm asking you to learn from others' stories. Remember a favorite children's story, book, or movie of someone overcoming the odds to be successful, the classic Hero's Journey.

- Why is it your favorite?

- What are some of the common elements?

- What do you learn that you can apply to launching your Big Idea or creating your New Reality?

EXPAND YOUR OPTIONS WITH "STRATAGEMS"

All cultures have stories about the hero overcoming obstacles. In Europe and the Americas, they are called fairy tales. In India, the Puranas. In Japan, koans. And in China, stratagems. For me, the *36 Stratagems*[32] are quite special. They are stories created and passed down over one thousand years of storytelling, and they are especially useful in a business setting when looking for ways to innovate.

Even if you aren't in the business world, why start from scratch when you can use another's story to get your creativity going? You can start here with some of the tried and true.

For example, one of the narratives is about how you partner with someone unexpected. This is how Microsoft created the Xbox.

- Who might you partner with, even competitors, outside of your current consideration to achieve success?

- Not sure who that might be? Ask:

  □ Who else benefits if you win?

  □ What can you offer them?

Another is about how you can coordinate resources or people who are typically not connected. Think Uber, AirBnb, Ebay. Due to technology, these organizations gather people together under one umbrella to provide a service. If any one individual attempted to launch their own transportation, lodging, or online service, it would be called a small business and would face all of the expenses related to it. Joining together spreads the risk and cost and enables individuals to join the service economy.

- Who could you coordinate?

  ◻ Customers? Experts? Employees? Regulators?

- As you explore these stratagems, what new ideas emerge?

- What can you apply from what you learn from these stories to your own project?

If you found this useful, a complete list of the thirty-six Chinese stratagems can be found at: https://outthinker.com/category/36-stratagems/.

 ## ASK THE EXPERT

Having just come from the business world in the last exercise, let's consider best practices. As a reminder from Chapter Eight (workbook), a best practice is an approach that is considered highly effective. Look for best practices in and out of your field by others who have tried something similar in the past.

Search the internet, of course, but don't be shy to call up THE person or company who has achieved a comparable goal. Right now, you are so small that your idea is not a threat to them. I used this strategy several times in consulting and was always delighted to hear, "Sure, I'd be willing to talk." I actually don't recall anyone ever saying "No." One tip, don't be sly about it:

1. Tell them what you are trying to accomplish.
2. Acknowledge that, in your research, their work was referenced several times, so you thought: *It never hurts to ask.*
3. Congratulate them on their accomplishments.
4. Ask if they'd be willing to allow you to interview them about their experience of creating success. You don't have to ask for their trade secrets, you just need to learn about their approach.

   ▪ What can you apply from what you learn about their experience to your own project?

   ▪ What ideas could you adopt and adapt?

 COLLABORATE AND WELCOME NEW MEMBERS

Be ready to welcome your new Supporters. Ask them:

   ▪ What draws you to the idea now?
   ▪ What have you learned in the past that you believe could make it even better?
   ▪ What unique talents do you bring that we should incorporate into implementation?
   ▪ Of these three implementation steps (be sure to give them some viable options), how would you like to be involved to ensure our completion?

CELEBRATE WITH MEANINGFUL RECOGNITION

Communicate your expectations on your path to meaningful recognition.

Ask:

- What will you recognize? Milestone accomplishments? Approaches to working that foster greater innovation and achievement?

- How will you celebrate your own accomplishments? Dark chocolate? A warm bath with scented candles? Downloading the latest single of your favorite artist?

- How does each of your Supporters prefer to be recognized and thanked?

CREATIVE WAYS TO APPRECIATE PEOPLE

People like to be acknowledged and so many ways exist. My team at Microsoft gave a quarterly award to recognize great collaboration, *The Red Baton*. It was a red, aluminum track and field relay baton engraved with each winner's name and the quarter that it was received. The red came from the chakra color that represents "tribe." The aluminum stood for a metal that is both strong and flexible. The baton represented the passing of information between colleagues.

- What can you use to create a fun and more meaningful celebration?

 ## THANK-YOU NOTES

Don't overlook the simple thank-you note. A handwritten note can go a long way to demonstrate appropriate appreciation for a meaningful contribution to launching your Big Idea or creating a New Reality. In fact, go beyond this. Occasionally, I would send thank-you notes to my team's individual family members to express gratitude for the support they gave their parents or partner. It not only surprised my team but also truly touched them that I included their family members in the gratitude.

- Who is it time to thank and what will you thank them for?

For additional ways to recognize people aside from financial rewards, you can read this article: "51 Ways to Reward Employees Without Money" (at https://www.americanexpress.com/en-us/business/trends-and-insights/articles/51-ways-to-reward-employees-without-money-1/).

CONCLUSION
¡BUEN CAMINO!

"Humankind has not woven the web of life. We are but one thread within it. Whatever we do to the web, we do to ourselves. All things are bound together. All things connect."
— Chief Seattle

Gracias! Thank you! If you have made it this far with me as your guide, you honor the approach the Camino has given to me and all of us. In these moments together, you *WE the Change* to bring your Big Idea or New Reality to life.

Celebrate your accomplishment! Return to that list you created of how you'd like to celebrate your own accomplishments and do one. As for me, you can count on the fact that I am raising a Dove dark chocolate in your honor.

Now, my friend, let's continue. Remember that, while you have completed the first steps to launch your Big Idea and create your New Reality, your journey continues. More support is available. You certainly aren't alone. Join your *WE the Change* community at www.wethechange.solutions.

Left to right: Savannah, Shannon, Fiona, and Joe
celebrate with a boot of Dove dark chocolate!

¡Buen Camino!

LESSONS OF
WE THE CHANGE

LESSON ONE: Anything Is Possible If You Just Say Yes

LESSON TWO: Know Where You Are Going

LESSON THREE: Know What You Are Leaving Behind

LESSON FOUR: Engage Your Supporters

LESSON FIVE: Pack Light

LESSON SIX: Commit to Going and Go!

LESSON SEVEN: Say What Needs to Be Said

LESSON EIGHT: Seek the Signals and Signposts

LESSON NINE: It Wouldn't Be a Pilgrimage If It Weren't Challenging

LESSON TEN: Face Your Dragons

LESSON ELEVEN: Count Your Blessings—Not Your Blisters!

Review Inquiry

Hey, it's Shannon here.

I hope you've enjoyed the book, finding it both useful and meaningful. I have a favor to ask you.

Would you consider giving it a rating wherever you bought the book? Online book stores are more likely to promote a work when they feel good about its content, and reader reviews are a great barometer for a book's quality.

If willing, please go to the website of wherever you bought the book, search for my name and the book title, and leave a review. Consider adding a picture of you holding the book. That increases the likelihood your review will be accepted!

Many thanks in advance,
Shannon Wallis

Will You Share the Love?
Get this book for a friend, associate, or family member!

If you have found this book valuable and know others who would find it useful, consider buying them a copy as a gift. Special bulk discounts are available if you would like your whole team or organization to benefit from reading this. Just contact Shannon at Shannon@CascadeLeadership.Solutions or Shannon's assistant, Carmen, at Carmen@CascadeLeadership.Solutions.

Would You Like Shannon Wallis to Speak to Your Organization?
Book Shannon Now!

Shannon accepts a limited number of speaking/coaching/training engagements each year. To learn how you can bring her message to your organization,

email Shannon@CascadeLeadership.Solutions.

ENDNOTES

1. Richard Beckhard, *Organization Development: Strategies and Models* (Reading, MA: Addison-Wesley, 1969). And Dannemiller, K. D. and R. W. Jacobs, "Changing the Way Organizations Change: A Revolution of Common Sense," *Journal of Applied Behavioral Science*, 28(4), pp. 480–498.

2. David Hoffeld, *The Science of Selling: Proven Strategies to Make Your Pitch, Influence Decisions, and Close the Deal* (Penguin Publishing Group, 2016).

3. Dr. Carol S. Dweck, *Mindset: The New Psychology of Success* (Random House, 2006).

4. "Path of Least Resistance," Wikipedia.

5. Robert Fritz, *The Path of Least Resistance: Learning to Become the Creative Force in Your Own Life* (Butterworth-Heinemann, 1994).

6. Malcolm Gladwell, *Outliers: The Story of Success* (Little, Brown and Company, 2009). In *Outliers*, Gladwell explains that reaching the 10,000-Hour Rule, which he considers the key to success in any field, is simply a matter of practicing a specific task that can be accomplished with twenty hours of work a week for ten years.

7. Erik Mazziotta, Difficult Conversations Workshop, Miami, Florida, December 15, 2012.

8. Patrick Lencioni, *The 5 Dysfunctions of a Team* (Jossey-Bass, 2002).

9. As stated in an article by Carleton, R. Nicholas: " 'fear of the unknown may be a, or possibly the, fundamental fear' underlying anxiety and therein neuroticism (Carleton, 2016; p. 39). Fear of the unknown (FOTU) will be defined herein as, 'an individual's propensity to experience fear caused by the perceived absence of information at any level of consciousness or point of processing'; relatedly, intolerance of uncertainty (IU) will be defined as, 'an individual's dispositional incapacity to endure the aversive response triggered by the perceived absence of salient, key, or sufficient information, and sustained by the associated

perception of uncertainty' " (Carleton, 2016; p. 31). "Into the unknown: A review and synthesis of contemporary models involving uncertainty." *Journal of Anxiety Disorders*, vol. 39, April 2016, pp. 30–43, doi:10.1016/j.janxdis.2016.02.007.

10. David Rock, "SCARF: A Brain-Based Model for Collaborating with and Influencing Others," *NeuroLeadership Journal*, no. one, 2008.

11. Sabine Leitner, "Modern Mythology," *New Acropolis Library*, August 8, 2014.

12. Joseph Campbell, *The Hero with a Thousand Faces* (Princeton University Press, 1968).

13. Catford, Lorna and Michael Ray, *The Path of the Everyday Hero: Drawing on the Power of Myth to Meet Life's Most Important Challenges*, p. 30 (G. P. Putnam's Sons, 1991).

14. Catford, Lorna and Michael Ray, *The Path of the Everyday Hero: Drawing on the Power of Myth to Meet Life's Most Important Challenges*, p. 27 (G. P. Putnam's Sons, 1991).

15. William Goldman, *The Princess Bride*, MGM Home Entertainment, 1987.

16. Joseph Campbell, *Joseph Campbell and The Power of Myth*. PBS, 1988.

17. David Rock, "SCARF: A Brain-Based Model for Collaborating with and Influencing Others," *NeuroLeadership Journal*, no. one, 2008.

18. Kaihan Krippendorff, *Outthink the Competition: How a New Generation of Strategists Sees Options Others Ignore* (John Wiley & Sons, Inc., 2011).

19. Kaihan Krippendorff, *Outthink the Competition: How a New Generation of Strategists Sees Options Others Ignore* (John Wiley & Sons, Inc., 2011).

20. Derek Sivers, "How to Start a Movement," TED, February 2010, https://www.ted.com/talks/derek_sivers_how_to_start_a_movement/transcript?language=en.

21. Kouzes, James M. and Barry Z. Posner, *The Leadership Challenge, 3rd ed.* (Jossey-Bass, 2002).

22. Kegan, Robert and Lisa Laskow Lahey, "Diagnosing Your Own Immunity to Change," *Immunity to Change: How to Overcome It and Unlock Potential in Yourself and Your Organization* (Harvard Business School Publishing Corporation, 2009), pp. 231–251.

23. Mind Tools Content Team, "Stakeholder Analysis: Winning Support for Your Projects," Mind Tools, www.mindtools.com/pages/article/newPPM_07.htm, and Project Management Institute, *A Guide to the Project Management Body of Knowledge (PMBOK® Guide)*, Newtown Square, PA, Project Management Institute, 2013, p. 397.

24. Goldsmith, Marshall, and Mark Reiter, *What Got You Here Won't Get You There: How Successful People Become Even More Successful* (Hachette Books, 2007).

25. Marcia Zina Mager, www.MarciaZinaMager.com.

26. Marianne Williamson, *A Return to Love: Reflections on the Principles of a Course in Miracles* (HarperCollins, 1996).

27. Suzy Welch, *10-10-10: 10 Minutes, 10 Months, 10 Years: A Life-Transforming Idea* (Scribner, 2009).

28. Ron Crossland, *Voice Lessons: Applying Science to the Art of Leadership Communication* (Ron Crossland, 2012). Ron Crossland actually refers to the "4 Fatal Flaws of Communication," starting with "Did they understand the message?"

29. "The Human Attention Span," Digital Information World, https://www.digitalinformationworld.com/2018/09/the-human-attention-span-infographic.html.

30. Erik Mazziotta, Difficult Conversations Workshop, Miami, Florida, December 15, 2012.

31. Catford, Lorna and Michael Ray, *The Path of the Everyday Hero: Drawing on the Power of Myth to Meet Life's Most Important Challenges*, pp. 19–21.

32. Kaihan Krippendorff, *Outthink the Competition* (John Wiley & Sons, Inc., 2011).

FURTHER READING

Berger, Warren. *A More Beautiful Question: The Power of Inquiry to Spark Breakthrough Ideas.* New York: Bloomsbury USA, 2014.

Bridges, William. *Managing Transitions: Making the Most of Change.* Addison-Wesley Publishing Company, 1991.

Bridges, William. *Transitions: Making Sense of Life's Changes.* Da Capo Press, 2004.

Brown, Brene. *The Gifts of Imperfection: Let Go of Who You Think You Are Supposed to Be and Embrace Who You Are.* Hazelden, 2010.

Cabrera, Beth. *Beyond Happy: Women, Work, and Well-Being.* Association for Talent Development Press, 2015.

Cameron, Julia. *The Artist's Way: A Spiritual Path to Higher Creativity.* Penguin Books, 1992.

Emerald, David. *The Power of TED: The Empowerment Dynamic.* Polaris Publishing, 2016.

Faith, Kimberly. *Your Lion Inside: Discover the Power Within and Live Your Fullest Life.* Advantage®, 2019.

Gawain, Shakti. *Creative Visualization.* Whatever Publishers, 1978.

Jaworski, Joseph. *Synchronicity: The Inner Path of Leadership.* Berrett-Koehler, 2007.

Kantor, David. *Reading the Room: Group Dynamics for Coaches and Leaders.* Jossey-Bass, 2012.

Kleiner, Art. *The Fifth Discipline Fieldbook.* Nicholas Brearley, 1994.

Kübler-Ross Elizabeth. *On Death and Dying.* Yomiuri Shinbunsha, 1972.

Leonard, George. *Mastery: The Keys to Success and Long-Term Fulfillment.* Plume, 1992.

Medina, John Baptist de. *Brain Rules: 12 Principles for Surviving and Thriving at Work, Home, and School.* Pear Press, 2014.

Price Waterhouse. *Change Integration Overview and Baseline Version 2.0.* Price Waterhouse World Firm Services BV, Inc., 1995.

Rock, David. *Your Brain at Work: Strategies for Overcoming Distraction, Regaining Focus, and Working Smarter All Day Long.* Harper Business, an Imprint of HarperCollins Publishers, 2009.

Senge, Peter M. *The Fifth Discipline.* New York: Doubleday, 1990.

Whitmore, John. *Coaching for Performance.* Nicholas Brealey, 1996.

ABOUT THE AUTHOR

Anything is possible—it's a phrase most people write off as a cliché. But not Shannon. Before she was a leadership consultant, before she was a senior executive at a Fortune 100 company, before she received her MBA from Duke, she was a young woman in a small town, from a humble home, with little hope of ever leaving. But she did leave and achieve, and she believes anything is possible. More importantly, Shannon believes you too can accomplish the remarkable, and she is here to help you make that happen. Bottom line—she's not satisfied with "what ifs" that lead to "only ifs," and you shouldn't be either.

As a leadership consultant, Shannon pushes and inspires leaders to model the exemplary leadership that can transform companies, organizations and communities. It's a job she loves, and it's given her the opportunity to work with remarkable people at incredible companies like Amazon, Coca-Cola, FedEx,

Grameen Foundation, Guidehouse, Microsoft, Nuestros Pequeños Hermanos, Trinity Education Foundation, United Planet, and Zillow.

But before she was helping senior leaders do the impossible, Shannon was one of them. At Microsoft, she became the first person to head up High Potential Leadership Development on a global level. How? By being the first person to both see the need and act on it. In the role, she led a global team of high-performers and managed a multi-million dollar budget. She also learned a lot; like, no matter where you work or where you live, exemplary leadership cascades through an organization and makes everyone better.

Shannon is also the proud mother of two teenage daughters. She's been happily married to her husband for twenty-two years and resides in Bellevue, WA, outside of Seattle. When she's not supporting clients and organizations to embrace their highest potential, you can find her traveling the globe, exploring cultures, meeting new friends, and seeking connection, community, and . . . chocolate.

Shannon can be reached at: www.wethechange.solutions.

CPSIA information can be obtained
at www.ICGtesting.com
Printed in the USA
FSHW021457170621